P9-EES-336

MY STORIES,
MY TIMES

MY STORIES, MY TIMES
JEAN CHRÉTIEN

TRANSLATED BY
SHEILA FISCHMAN
AND DONALD WINKLER

RANDOM HOUSE CANADA

PUBLISHED BY RANDOM HOUSE CANADA

Copyright © 2018 Jean Chrétien Professional Corp.
English translation copyright © 2018 Sheila Fischman and Donald Winkler

All rights reserved under International and Pan-American Copyright Conventions.
No part of this book may be reproduced in any form or by any electronic or
mechanical means, including information storage and retrieval systems, without
permission in writing from the publisher, except by a reviewer, who may quote
brief passages in a review. Published in 2018 by Random House Canada, a division
of Penguin Random House Canada Limited, Toronto. Distributed in Canada
by Penguin Random House Canada Limited, Toronto.

www.penguinrandomhouse.ca

Random House Canada and colophon are registered trademarks.

Library and Archives Canada Cataloguing in Publication

Chrétien, Jean, 1934–
[Mes histoires. English]
    My stories, my times / Jean Chrétien ; translated by Sheila Fischman
and Donald Winkler.

Translation of: Mes histoires.
Issued in print and electronic formats.
ISBN 978-0-7352-7734-2
eBook ISBN 978-0-7352-7735-9

    1. Chrétien, Jean, 1934– —Anecdotes. 2. Canada—Politics and
government—1963-1984. 3. Canada—Politics and government—
1984–1993. 4. Canada—Politics and government—1993–2006. 5. Prime
ministers—Canada—Anecdotes. I. Title. II. Title: Mes histoires. English

FC636.C47A3 2018b   971.064'8092   C2018-903533-1
                                                 C2018-903534-X

Book design by Five Seventeen
Cover photograph by Fred Chartrand

Printed and bound in Canada

10 9 8 7 6 5 4 3 2 1

Penguin
Random House
RANDOM HOUSE CANADA

To my wife, Aline

To my children:
France, Hubert, and Michel

To my grandchildren:
Olivier, Maximilien, Philippe, Jacqueline, and Katherine

To my great-grandchildren:
William, Gaia, Athena, Amédeo, Sacha, and Ariane

CONTENTS

☙

FOREWORD BY JOE CLARK

Politicians are best known for the things we did—or didn't do—in office, but we have afterlives too, which, among other advantages, allow the opportunity to recall, and sometimes reflect upon, things we saw and heard and felt during and after our privileged days in public office. By definition, such observations are bound to be personal and reflect a point of view, but they can also provide invaluable context to decisions and events that others can know only at a distance. All of the dry and distant facts of history have a story, often a human story, which can be as important and informative as the event itself. Canada is fortunate that Jean Chrétien, at eighty-four, and fifty-five years after his first election to the House of Commons, is publishing some of his reflections on people and events that shaped our history.

By a tradition as old as parliamentary democracy, the distance between the government and the opposition benches in Canada's House of Commons is "two swords and one inch apart." That distance symbolizes and encourages debate that is vigorous and adversarial but not fatal—to the participants, or to the country. For more than two decades, Jean Chrétien and I sat two sword lengths across from one another in Canada's Parliament.

On some issues, we had deep disagreements—probably the most important concerned certain provisions of the Constitution Act of 1982 which, as Minister of Justice, he introduced. As Leader of the Opposition, I forced a very long parliamentary debate, winning time for televised public hearings, followed by a successful reference to the Supreme Court, resulting ultimately in amendments that improved the proposed changes. In the end, we both voted for what was called "patriation," and for the amended Charter of Rights and Freedoms—but the two of us still disagree on the larger implications for Canadian unity and integrity of the way our constitution was changed during that critical period.

Jean Chrétien and I were each shaped by one other unique opportunity. Each of us was elected to lead our national political party in a time when national parties reached habitually beyond their base and sought to embrace and understand the whole country, all its people and all its parts. We are both the product of an era when contact with voters was direct, face to face, often on contentious ground—and those actual human exchanges could temper the influence of advisers or pollsters, or sophisticated interest groups, or ideologues.

Those reality checks seem more elusive today, and the distance greater between citizens and politicians, in an era when leaders' interactions with voters are more often electronic than personal, or by way of rallies where citizens are screened before entry. I say that not as elegy, but as explanation of the vital direct access that leaders of our earlier time were privileged to have with the lives and hopes and fears of fellow Canadians.

One of the unexpected privileges of being a party leader was the frankness with which individual citizens would tell you their story. They may never vote for you, but they know that, sometime, you might make decisions which will affect their lives, so they want you to understand their problems and their hopes. And if your pores are open, you learn a lot in those encounters.

As time went on, Jean and I both came to understand that just as in Canada there can be a rare frankness from citizen to leader, so, in this complex international climate, there is often a comparable openness between leaders of different countries. There are so few people with whom a president or prime minister can be frank that they sometimes confide in visiting peers, when the chemistry is right. The "little guy from Shawinigan" is pretty good at human chemistry, and his reflections on international conversations add extra dimensions to our understanding of international events.

Most Canadians are still framed by where we come from and, in many cases—Shawinigan, for example, or High River— our hometown is only a tiny part of the country, or the world, or the era in which we have to function. That poses a special challenge for political leaders, because our profession requires knitting different communities together, rather than focusing more narrowly.

Thus, two questions arise. First, how do leaders learn about our remarkably diverse country, and complicated world? As much as possible by immersion in it, by reaching out, by being open-minded, especially when that's hard. We all fall short; but we learn, as we grow.

So the second question is: What can former leaders teach?

The best historians and social scientists gather a rich and deep and wide array of "evidence" that is considered objective. But necessarily, their invaluable assessments are most often from the outside looking in. The dimension that former leaders can offer is reflection and perspective—and often simply stories—from the inside looking back.

I cannot vouch for the accuracy of all of the reflections in this collection. As a partisan, reading an opposing partisan, I would naturally dispute some of them. But my purpose is neither fact-checking nor peer review. I'm interested in having Canada's human stories known.

Among his indisputable qualities, Jean Chrétien is a natural storyteller. His ear and eye often catch nuances that a strict reading or recording might miss, and then his instinct or experience fills in blanks. These are informed personal reflections on significant times and events that take us beyond what we know. They are also very human, and will help enrich readers' sense of our country and our world. And they are often the opposite of the careful scripting that caricatures politics and government today.

Many political leaders write books on their way to office— or to put their own spin on what happened when they were there. Of course, one doesn't get political leaders without some spin, but these stories seem to me to express a more interesting dimension than ego or ambition. If there's an ulterior motive, it is to pass along some of the lessons learned in a long life that has been, by any standard, extraordinary and informative. I commend this book and—from two swords' lengths away, thank my former adversary for one more service to our country.

PREFACE

We live at a time when the fate of our liberal democratic system is being intensely questioned, autocracies appear to be on the march, and too many people speak despairingly and cynically about the ability of the democratic countries to provide good government for their citizens.

I spent fifty years of my life working in politics as a member of Parliament, a minister, leader of the opposition, and prime minister. Throughout that period I developed a profound faith in the merits of our Canadian democracy.

I have witnessed great progress in our society, where elected representatives of different backgrounds and political convictions have worked to build a more prosperous, healthier, better educated, and more tolerant Canada based on a respect for due process, the rule of law, and protections for the weakest in our society.

We still have a long way to go, but the journey to the Promised Land was never meant to be a destination but just that, a journey.

What follows is a series of observations, stories, experiences, and anecdotes, some serious, others less so. It reflects my deep appreciation for the opportunity I was given to be part of this great journey, not to make our world perfect but to try to make it better.

It is written in the hope that people of all ages will read it and gain an understanding of the richness of the human dimension in politics, the nobility of its purpose, the diversity of the society in which we live, and the strength of the human fabric that binds us together.

❦

Sometimes, after a good supper, I become talkative, and I'm asked to tell stories about my long political career. One night my grandson Olivier told me that I should write down all my stories and anecdotes, with their mingling of the serious and the humorous, and that if I didn't do so they would get lost. I told him that I wasn't a writer, but that I'd think about it.

About the same time, a friend gave me a book that made up my mind, that became my stimulus. After leaving politics, the eighth prime minister of Canada, Sir Robert Borden, became bored with his life and, to amuse himself, decided to write letters that chronicled the political and social life of the country, just for himself, to be stashed away in a drawer. Then about thirty years after his death, his grandson made a very interesting book out of them, published under the title *Letters to Limbo*. I thought it was a good precedent, and I decided to pick up my pen to share these memories with my children, my grandchildren, and my great-grandchildren. Over the past year I've spent many hours with paper, my pen, and my memories. Even when I tell a story that some have heard once or twice before, writing it down has called new details to mind, even years after the fact.

Finally, I'd like to warn my readers, and to beg their indulgence for certain passages that may seem strange and/or old-fashioned if looked at through today's eyes, but that simply reflect, to my mind, the rites, the mentalities, the values, and the atmosphere of our society in times past.

I am not writing my memoirs, or a history book. In fact, I'm having fun. When I'm tired of observing the surrealist vagaries of President Trump, and of listening to his nonsense, I recover my serenity at the work table. Aline and my grandchildren persuaded me to write a book with no other ambition than perhaps to entertain. . . . And here it is!

1

AN UNSUNG HERO

H old on! I remember. . . .
Now that I have more free time, maybe I should do
some writing. So, let's get started.

On December 17, 1996, we suddenly learned that terrorists belonging to the Marxist revolutionary group Tupac
Amaru had taken hostage three hundred people, including
three ambassadors, at the Japanese official residence in Lima,
Peru. Our ambassador, Anthony Vincent, whom I'd known
for some time, was one of them. My people kept me up to
date, and I followed with concern the development of this
dramatic hostage-taking.

At a certain point during the long siege, which lasted more
than five months, the terrorists let the three ambassadors go
in order to negotiate with Peruvian authorities, on condition
that they would return once their mission was completed.

In other words, at the end of their talks with the Peruvian
authorities, the three ambassadors, theoretically, were to return
and make a report to the terrorists, their captors, who were still

inside the Japanese residence. In the end, only the Canadian ambassador decided to go back. But his superiors in Ottawa, with whom he had been talking, saw the tremendous risk Anthony Vincent was taking, and said that he had to discuss the matter with me, his prime minister.

The conversation I then had with Ambassador Vincent will remain, to the end of my days, one of my most moving memories. On the telephone that January night in 1997, Anthony Vincent, in few words, very clearly and very calmly explained the situation to me. He told me that his two colleagues had decided not to return to the residence, and that he, on the contrary, wanted to respect the word he had given, which was also his country's word. Under the circumstances he felt he had no other choice. We talked for a few minutes more, and he told me again that he intended to go back, unless I ordered him not to do so. I told him that I would respect his decision. "Well," he said, "I'm returning to the Japanese residence to meet with the terrorists." I told him that he was a very brave and very honourable man, and that Canada was proud of him. I then added that I would pray for him, and I wished him good luck.

He went back to report to his jailers. He was again released and he again kept his word. Everything ended well, in spectacular and tragic fashion. The siege had lasted 126 days when a commando of armed Peruvian soldiers entered the Japanese ambassador's residence through a network of tunnels that had been dug during the long hostage-taking. In total, seventy-two hostages were freed after the assault, which, though widely hailed as a success, did cost the life of one hostage, two Peruvian commandos, and all the members of the Marxist revolutionary group, Tupac Amaru.

After this incredible adventure, Anthony Vincent returned to Canada to continue serving his adopted country. In 1998, the government gave him a well-deserved promotion as Canada's ambassador to the Spanish government in Madrid.

Sadly, he was not able to pursue his exceptionally promising career very long, for he died prematurely in 1999.

Whatever interpretations may have been advanced on the precise role of each of the players during the hostage crisis, for me Anthony Vincent will remain an unsung hero who did honour to his profession and his country. Rather than debating the appropriateness of erecting a monument to the victims of communism but not those of capitalism, perhaps we could agree to commemorate unknown heroes like Anthony Vincent.

2

BECAUSE BUTTER IS BUTTER

It's 1955. The graduating class of the Trois-Rivières Seminary, of which I am part, is on its way to the Quebec legislature to pay a visit to a distinguished alumnus of our school, Premier Maurice Duplessis.

Once we are facing him, each of us steps forward, utters his name, and holds out his hand. When my turn comes, he asks me to repeat my name. I reply, "Jean Chrétien." "Chrétien?" he says. "Yes, Chrétien of Shawinigan." "Your father is Wellie Chrétien?" "Yes, M. Duplessis." "Your grandfather was François Chrétien, mayor of Saint-Étienne-des-Grès?" "Yes, monsieur le premier ministre." "So you're a 'goddamn red.'" Instantly, in the minds of my friends, I became an enthusiastic supporter of the Liberal Party.

The next to extend his hand to M. Duplessis was my friend Jean Pelletier, who, after introducing himself, said, "Monsieur le premier ministre, I would like to inform you that your alma mater is not respecting your laws and is forcing us to eat

margarine instead of butter. And therefore acting illegally."
"Not possible," answered the premier.

Then I pulled out of my jacket pocket the margarine that we had carefully wrapped in waxed paper and handed it to M. Duplessis.

Immediately after the meeting, Duplessis sent our margarine to the ministry of agriculture to have it analyzed by experts.

Duplessis had passed a law declaring the use of margarine illegal, in order to protect the farmers, because its consumption cost the butter producers dearly. As the premier preferred to protect the farmers, who supported him in great numbers, rather than to help the urban consumers who were significantly less supportive of him, he had decided to make selling the product illegal all over Quebec. A rather radical measure, if you ask me!

You should have seen the look on *le Chef*'s face when he took the little package. As for Pelletier and me, we were proud of our coup.

After listening to "Maurice," during what was probably an hour, telling us all sorts of stories, we left, delighted to have met the most renowned former student of our college. He may have been too conservative for many of us, but he was also a charming man, witty and cultivated—and a collector of Quebec paintings. It was a memorable day.

Towards the end of the afternoon, the Department of Agriculture informed Monsieur Duplessis that indeed, the product they had analyzed was margarine.

Immediately, the premier phoned Msgr. Ouellette, the seminary's superior. Pelletier and I would have loved to hear the sermon that Duplessis must have delivered to the poor man. It would have been a very painful moment for someone so dignified and so proud.

The next morning, when Jean Pelletier and I sat down to breakfast in the seminary's refectory, someone brought us a half pound of butter. For the rest of the year, we never saw a hint of a piece of margarine. Because in the end, butter is butter, and nothing else.

3

THE FOUR PILLARS OF FINANCE

While Bill Clinton was president of the United States, he made drastic changes to the rules governing the financial sector on Wall Street. It was what was called the great deregulation of financial services.

Since the time of President Franklin D. Roosevelt, bankers were bankers, insurers were insurers, bank business was bank business, and brokers were brokers: there was no way to amalgamate those four sectors. Clinton's green light for Wall Street to deregulate the financial sector resulted in huge mergers and paved the way for the 2008 financial disaster. In the beginning, though, there was euphoria in New York and elsewhere in the finance world.

Canadian bankers, obviously, wanted to join the dance of these enormous amalgamations. All indications are that if we had done the same thing, only two or three Canadian banks would have survived the operation.

Those of my ministers who were close to the business sector wanted us to follow the lead of the Americans, but I thought on the contrary that the independence of the four pillars of finance, each of which had been separate from the others since the 1930s, had served us well and should be maintained. Bay Street, having learned that I was the problem, delegated Matthew Barrett, CEO of the Bank of Montreal, to try to make me change my mind. I knew Matthew well; he was an Englishman, very likable, and also very good at his job.

We met in the Office of the Prime Minister on Parliament Hill, where he explained in detail the many reasons why the government ought to allow the amalgamation of the banks.

"There is no great Canadian bank that can rival the great American, British, French, German, Swiss, Japanese banks," he told me. To which I replied, "How is it then that the world's biggest banks are in Japan and they're all bankrupt, or just about," which was true in 1999.

After a few minutes of fruitless discussion, he at last came out with his final argument. "Prime Minister, you must permit the amalgamation of the banks, because it's in the national interest." I responded, "If we must act solely in the country's national interest, then let's do so together. We, the government ministers, all work entirely in the national interest, and we do so for salaries much lower than those of bank presidents, and with no stock options as rewards. So, if you bankers will do the same, and not exercise a single one of your options, we'll go ahead. It will be done entirely in everyone's national interest." I don't think he found me very funny, and he left, disappointed, to inform his friends of my decision, which was final.

After the crisis in the financial world in October 2008, Canadian banks came to be viewed all over the world as the sector's shining stars.

Since that time, I have enjoyed telling bank presidents who are being praised on all sides for the way their institutions have performed, that I am very happy for them. And I add what they probably don't tell their admirers, that they owe their success to the government that stopped them from jumping off a bridge!

They no doubt profited less than they would have if there had been an amalgamation and they had exercised their options. The personal savings they pocketed may not be as impressive as they hoped, but the country and its financial sector are doing very well.

4

TONY BLAIR AND THE WAR IN IRAQ

At the end of August 2002, I spent more than an hour and a half with President George W. Bush in Detroit, discussing the need to declare war on Saddam Hussein's Iraq.

Bush's main argument revolved around the huge quantity of weapons of mass destruction Saddam possessed, some of which he had used against the Kurds in northwestern Iraq.

I was of the opinion that the evidence for Hussein's possession of these terrible arms was not very convincing, and that in any case the president would have to obtain the approval of the United Nations before proceeding; if not, Canada and many other countries would not support him.

A few weeks later, at a Commonwealth meeting in South Africa, following the afternoon session Tony Blair and I went to the hotel bar for a beer and took the opportunity to have a private talk. He tried to persuade me to support him and George W. in their determination to go to war with Iraq.

What surprised me most in this conversation was that rather than focusing his argument on the weapons of mass destruction, as George W. had done, Blair insisted rather on the fact that we absolutely had to get rid of Saddam Hussein because he was a ruthless tyrant, and he pushed this idea with multiple examples of the horrors of which Saddam was guilty.

I replied that if we planned on getting rid of all those leaders that we thought were unworthy to rule their countries, he and I ought first to take a good look at the nations of the Commonwealth; and that, reasonably, we should surely begin by intervening in Zimbabwe and removing Mugabe from power before going into Iraq to chase out Saddam.

He replied immediately that there was an important difference between Saddam and Mugabe. "Tony," I replied, "there is indeed a tremendous difference. Mugabe has no oil." He went white in the face, furious with me, and for many months our relations were no longer the same.

What I find sad in this affair is the enormous price he had to pay in his own country for this disastrous decision, when in my opinion he had been a very good prime minister. During his years in power, Great Britain had shone brightly on the world stage. In the end he had to leave his post amid a huge controversy that fourteen years later haunts him still.

I think that's a pity, because a politician's career is not only demanding, it can also be very tough and sometimes thankless. We know when we decide to go into politics that we will have to live with our decisions for a long time after our retirement . . . in fact, till the end of our days.

5

MY ROCK OF GIBRALTAR

Commentators do not always understand the role, often hidden and yet at times crucial, that spouses play in the policies put forward by a prime minister. From the start of my political career, Aline was at my side, even though at the beginning she was only twenty-six years old. She always had an enormous influence on the decisions I made during my forty years in political life. It's not for nothing that I always said that she was my Rock of Gibraltar.

For example, during the period leading up to the 1995 budget, the famous exercise in austerity that enabled us to balance the federal budget for the first time in decades, the officials in the Finance Department proposed combining the incomes of couples in order to establish which would qualify for an old age pension. So, for example, if a husband had a very high income, his wife would not receive the cheque of some four hundred dollars per month. This would mean that many wives not working outside the home would lose the federal government's monthly cheque that often represented their only personal income.

At dinner with a couple we knew, I told Aline and her friend that the finance minister intended to include this measure in his budget, and that the idea worried me. The two women's reactions were instant and unambiguous.

"That's just stupid," they said to me. "What an injustice for all those women who stayed home to raise their children and take care of their family! They all look forward to the happy day each month when they at last receive a few dollars of their very own, that they can spend as they see fit. They can invite a friend for cake and coffee in a restaurant, they can buy something for themselves—all without having to ask their husbands for money. You men don't know how horrible it is always having to ask . . . Not all husbands are as kind as you two"—and so forth.

I have to say that I sank into my armchair and humbly endured this assault from two women who at that moment were in a position to tell the government, directly and unambiguously, what they thought. The next day I informed the finance minister that no, this proposal could not appear in the budget.

My finance minister was not very happy with my decision and he sent his adviser Peter Nicholson to 24 Sussex one Saturday to express his displeasure. The budget would soon go to press and they were awaiting my approval. Nicholson informed me that to be comfortable with his budget, Paul

Martin needed this measure, and that he might have to resign if I didn't agree to his demand. I then said to Peter, "I've always dreamed of being my own finance minister, and I would be delighted to read the budget myself."

Not only did the finance minister not resign, but he continued to fulfil his duties for seven more years, understanding very well that, in the end, the prime minister always has the last word.

Another instance where Aline's involvement in my political career was decisive took place during the biannual Liberal Party convention in the year 2000. I had decided, after the 1997 election, that after four years as prime minister I would leave political life at the respectable age of sixty-six. Aline was in complete agreement, because in her opinion thirty-seven years of public life was quite enough for me and, even more definitely, for her. I had not publicly announced my decision to leave politics, and as my government's popularity remained high, there were many supporters who wanted me to remain in place. On the other hand, there were some who felt that I had completed my task, and that the time had come for me to pass the baton.

And so, during the Ottawa convention, some impatient individuals behaved in a way that displeased Aline. She found their attitude inappropriate and disrespectful, given our long period of public service dating back to 1963. I left the convention with the clear support of the great majority of delegates, and Aline and I went to thank a group of my principal associates, many of whom urged me to try for a third mandate.

I told them that I would not do so because I had promised Aline that I would retire at the end of 2001, period. At that point Aline excused herself because she had to return to 24 Sussex to greet the delegates from my riding of Saint-Maurice, and she told me not to delay because our guests had to return to Shawinigan.

Aline then left the room, closing the door behind her, only to reappear immediately, her hand still on the door-knob. And, looking around at all of us, she said (in English) loudly and clearly, "Four more years." What a surprise! Amid the stupefaction that followed, everyone rose spontaneously to give her an enthusiastic ovation. That was how I decided not to resign but instead to throw myself into a quest for a third mandate, which turned out to be my most satisfying.

From December 2000 until my retirement in December 2003, a monthly Gallup poll consistently awarded the Liberal Party 50 to 60 percent of voters' support. The time has perhaps come at last for me to thank the impatient "Martinists" for having upset Aline that day because—to give just one example—if they had not, we would have gone to war in Iraq.

6

NATO: FROM SUMMIT TO SUMMIT

O ne of the most interesting parts of a prime minister's
work on the international scene is the opportunity to
participate in the G7 and NATO meetings.

A few weeks after my swearing in, I found myself at the
NATO summit in Brussels. It was January 9, 1994, the height
of the conflict in the former Yugoslavia, and our troops were
stuck inside the Srebrenica enclave. As this was the conflict's
hot spot, the Americans and British had proposed heavy
bombardments there, which would have endangered our soldiers on the ground. Their mandate had already been extended,
and we were in fact awaiting news on who would be replacing
them as peacekeepers in this part of the future Bosnia.

Bill Clinton and John Major were very insistent, but we
Canadians thought it would be preferable not to bomb,
especially since the troops would soon be leaving. As NATO
decisions always have to be unanimous, I held my ground,
even telling Bill Clinton that if he was so determined to
bomb he should do it when there were American soldiers on

the ground. Now, at this point our southern neighbours had not sent any troops to the combat zone. I don't think Bill was very happy when I told him he was "ready to fight to the last Canadian soldier. . . ."

On the other hand, he was more appreciative of my cooperation three years later at the NATO summit in Madrid, in July 1997. The day before the meeting opened, I had arrived at the reception desk of the hotel where we were staying, and I saw Bill and Hillary Clinton in conference with Jacques Chirac. There was tension in the air; they all looked worried, and there was no hint of a smile on any of their faces. After the French president left, Bill beckoned to me to come and join them. The problem that was troubling them was rather complicated: all the countries of the former Soviet Union wanted to join NATO, and Chirac thought that we needed to act quickly. He was emphatic that we should immediately accept nine of them. I was inclined to agree. Clinton, on the other hand, thought that we should proceed slowly, because he was afraid that Yeltsin, the Russian president, would be weakened if things moved too fast, and in the end I came to the conclusion that he was probably right. He told me, "You Canadians have to find us a solution." I said that I would think it over that night, and that I would see Chirac before the morning session.

The situation was difficult for Chirac. He had just lost the legislative elections in his country, and he now had to deal with a government made up of political factions other than his own. The foreign affairs minister who had accompanied him to Madrid was Hubert Védrine, named by the new prime minister, Lionel Jospin of the Socialist Party. In those circumstances, the French president could not easily change his position. When the thorny subject came up on the agenda, I spoke up claiming that the communiqué was different in French than in English and had to be rewritten. Everyone understood the manoeuvre, and Clinton asked the assembly to mandate me, together with the NATO Secretary General Javier Solana, to draw up a new text during the lunch break. My suggestion was that we immediately accept Poland and the Czech Republic, then Romania and Slovenia, and finally the three Baltic countries; all this over a period of several years. The Canadians participated in the writing of the decision, and all was approved at the end of the afternoon session.

On leaving, Clinton generously told my staff that I was a good lawmaker. Jacques Chirac, having a drink later with his old friend Jean Pelletier, both of them founding directors and for many years members of the International Association of Francophone Mayors, admitted that he'd painted himself into a corner, and that his friend Chrétien had got him out of it. All of which proves that having two official languages can sometimes be very useful when you least expect it.

7

DO YOUR DUTY!

Everyone says that if you do something popular during your mandate, people will remember and express their thanks by voting for you at the next election. My experience tells me that this is far from a certainty, and that sometimes all you get is a chance to show a certain humility.

In the October 1993 election, my party enjoyed tremendous success in the Maritime Provinces, winning thirty-one of the thirty-two seats existing at the time. I was very proud, and in 1995 took the opportunity to make my appreciation known in a highly visible way. Canada was host of the G7 meeting, and various cities were eager to receive the heads of state and governments of the United States, France, Great Britain, Germany, Japan, and Italy. What's more, I had persuaded my colleagues to open up our meeting to Russia's Boris Yeltsin, turning the G7 into the G8.

To thank the voters of Nova Scotia, where we'd taken every riding, I selected Halifax, which turned out to be a very fine choice. The weather was good, the hospitality excellent, the G7/G8 leaders who arrived at the Dartmouth military airport came by boat, most of them having sailed across beautiful Halifax Harbour. They were greeted by enthusiastic crowds on the wharves of the Nova Scotia capital. Of the ten G7 summits in which I participated, this one was the most relaxed. Unusually, the heads of state and government leaders mingled freely with the crowds in the Halifax streets, and it all ended with a superb performance by the Cirque du Soleil. Of course, that was long before 9/11, and the Twin Towers were still standing. . . .

One incident made a great impression on me: a worker with the Cirque told me that he would like to meet the British prime minister, John Major, because his father had been a companion and friend of John's father when they both worked for a circus in their youth. Who'd have thought that the father of the British prime minister had once had a career in the circus!

That week put Halifax on the map, thanks to the flawless unfolding of this important summit in the international spotlight. I was of course delighted with this success, and convinced that at the next federal election, the people of the beautiful city of Halifax and the rest of Nova Scotia's population would support us by way of thanks. No way! Imagine my surprise on the evening of the June 1997 elections, when we lost all eleven seats that we'd won in 1993.

Those who, like me, thought that the voters of Nova Scotia would thank us had miscalculated. What I learned was that given the opportunity, voters are more eager to show their disappointment than their gratitude. It's clear that they had not appreciated the recent unemployment insurance reforms, and that the tremendous success of the first de facto G8 summit played no role in their decision.

Happily, in my last election in the year 2000, these same voters changed their minds again, and gave us eight victories out of a possible eleven across the province. I concluded that in politics, as in life, it's most important to do one's duty, whatever the circumstances.

8

NEWFOUNDLAND: A GREAT DIPLOMATIC VICTORY

During my long political career, I often went to the province of Newfoundland and Labrador, and I have to say, I had a terrific time there. The landscape is always beautiful, the fjords are majestic, the rivers fast-flowing and spectacular, and above all, the people are lively and direct. Campaigning there was not work for me; it was like visiting cousins who are glad to see you. As Newfoundlanders are very colourful people, I have all sorts of interesting stories to tell, but one in particular comes to mind.

During the 1993 electoral period, I was faced with the problem of cod overfishing. The government had been forced to institute a moratorium on cod fishing, which undermined that much more the already weak economy of what was then the poorest province in Confederation. International law gave Canada sovereignty over a two-hundred-mile zone off our coasts. We had legal control over fishing in this zone. No one in Canada was allowed to go there to fish for cod, but Spanish and Portuguese fishing boats operating just outside the territorial waters of our famous two-hundred-mile zone continued to fish at will, thereby cancelling out, to all intents and purposes, the Canadian moratorium.

Canadian fishers were prevented from fishing in order to allow the stock to replenish itself, but this sacrifice was pointless if the Spanish and Portuguese continued their depletion of the fish stocks. My impulsive comrade-in-arms Brian Tobin convinced us that we had to make an electoral promise: that if re-elected we would put an end to this unjust situation.

Tobin, who had become my minister of fisheries, then took the file in hand, and the Spanish and Portuguese were advised that they had to follow the example of the Canadians to enable the cod to return to the waters of the continental shelf, which extended more than two hundred miles.

It was an epic dispute. Refusal of foreign countries to stop fishing. Threats to seize their vessels. Diplomatic crisis with the European Community, Portugal, and Spain. Debate within the United Nations. Division inside the Canadian cabinet: the ministers of the departments of Foreign Affairs and National Defence versus the minister of Fisheries.

I believed that it was the duty of any country bordering on the ocean to protect its fisheries within the two-hundred-mile limit. But in this case the continental shelf extended beyond the two hundred miles, and so to achieve our goal of successfully protecting the resource, we would have to use any and all means at our disposal. I gave Tobin my full support.

Thus began the episode misnamed "the Turbot War," which ended up with the Canadian Coast Guard boarding and searching the Spanish ship *Estai* by force. Tense negotiations in Brussels enabled us to defuse the crisis at the time.

Given the illegal fishing of the Spanish and Portuguese, we had to be firm, and I organized a special meeting of the cabinet for Good Friday. As Parliament was not sitting that week, I made a tour of Western Canada with Aline. When we were back home, and both rather tired after the tour, Aline said to me, "At last we can relax, because it's Easter weekend, and we have nothing planned until Tuesday." I replied, "I'm not so sure. Things may not be as restful as you'd like, because tomorrow I'm declaring war on Spain!" Of course, that was a bit of a joke, but Aline took it seriously. I had explained the tense situation involving Spain, but I didn't believe that in the end there would be an escalation that would lead to conflict. When I left the house to go to the cabinet meeting, Aline said that she had not slept all night. As I had only been trying to make a joke, I apologized. She, quite rightly, didn't find it very funny. Often politics is harder on the spouse and the children than on the prime minister himself.

The diplomatic controversy that erupted when we announced our decision was enormous. We had offended not only the Spanish and Portuguese governments, but the entire European Union and even the Americans. No one looked favourably on our defiant stand against a way of life that had existed for some decades. It all ended up before the United Nations in New York. Brian Tobin was Canada's standard bearer in the affair, and he was charged with defending our position before the UN General Assembly. During the boarding of the *Estai* by our coast guard, the Spanish sailors had jettisoned their nets, dropping them deep into the sea, but our agents had succeeded in retrieving them. They quickly saw why the Spanish sailors had acted in this way. Inside the regulation net there was another net with a much smaller mesh, a kind of net that was strictly forbidden by international regulations everywhere in the world. Tobin decided to exhibit the illegal nets, which he had hoisted with the aid of two cranes behind the United Nations headquarters. It was a stunning gesture, typical of the flamboyant Tobin; however, it was a gesture to which the foreign affairs minister objected. Tobin had to call me to ask my permission. I found it all very interesting, but there was the danger of it becoming a spectacular fiasco. And so I allowed Tobin to go ahead but at his own risk. It was understood that if the whole thing was a flop, he would pay the price. The European Union's commissioner responsible for fisheries, Emma Bonino, launched a furious attack against Canada, and when it was Tobin's turn, he was absolutely brilliant in his reply. Finally, he invited everyone to go and view the nets on the docks behind the huge UN headquarters. It was a knockout punch, and it ended the debate. Madam Commissioner took the first plane back to Brussels.

Peter Jennings, a Canadian who was then the most popular journalist on American television, told me that the ten-storey-high display of nets by the water in New York was the most spectacular theatrical gesture he had ever seen. Although this unorthodox way of proceeding had made me uneasy at first, I was very happy with the outcome, and I warmly congratulated my friend Brian.

After talks that went on for months, involving the United Nations, the European Commission, and all the countries with an interest in fishing on the high seas, international law was amended, and since then the countries whose continental shelf extends beyond the two-hundred-mile limit have the power to enforce their rules to protect species on the extended continental shelf. All things considered, this was a great diplomatic victory for Canada. What began as an electoral promise that might have been difficult to keep, ended with a change in international law.

The persistence of a determined minister enabled Canada to gain a stunning victory on the world stage. Thank you, my friend Brian!

Since that time, even with sophisticated satellite surveillance, the issue remains a concern. Rogue ships continue to play cat-and-mouse with the surveillance authorities, tacking back and forth between international waters and the no-fishing zone. What changed with this crisis, however, was that now the whole world knew that well-mannered Canada did not hesitate to show its teeth when it was a matter of legitimately defending the livelihood of its fishers.

9

THE GUIBORD AFFAIR

I n recent years religion has once again become politically
controversial in Quebec, and elsewhere in Canada too.
The debate over the extent of reasonable accommodation to
other religions may have begun not far from my home ground,
in Hérouxville, a very quiet little village where no Muslim has
ever lived. The famous municipal ruling that caused so much
ink to flow was proposed by a citizen who had worked in
Saudi Arabia and, it seems, wanted more or less to have some
fun. He was the most astonished person in the world to be
suddenly assailed by groups and journalists from all over the
world, as far away as Australia.

All of this leads me to the Guibord affair, which I learned
about long ago in a church law class taught by a notary named
Giroux, brother-in-law of Cardinal Maurice Roy of Quebec.
This little man, with his tousled hair, attacked the Catholic
Church with tirades so effective that they had to be heard
to be believed. For us, seminary graduates with bachelor's
degrees who for years had been taught only by professors

who were also priests, it was priceless: we spontaneously applauded.

During the 1890s there was an organization in Quebec called the Institut canadien, whose members were quite radical for their time. In opposition to the ultramontanes, they advocated the absolute separation of church and state, and supported other measures controversial at the time, including the European model of economic and political liberalism, which was outlawed by the Church. At the end of the nineteenth century, this was all very serious and important for many people. (Furthermore, there exists not far from the National Assembly in the Upper Town of Quebec City a rather impressive building where I spent some time when I was studying at Laval University, and which bears the name "l'Institut Canadien.")

Some of the most vocal members of the radical group were excommunicated. Such was the case for poor Joseph Guibord, a member of the Montreal chapter of the Institut. On his death, his family wanted to bury him in the family plot in the Montreal Catholic cemetery, but Msgr. Bourget, bishop of the diocese, was opposed. What a controversy! And so the family had Guibord's mortal remains interred in the city's Protestant cemetery, and went to court against the Bishop of Montreal. The lower court decided in favour of the Guibord family and ordered the diocese to allow entry to the body of the excommunicated member, so that he could be buried alongside the other members of his family.

This became a huge controversy when the clergy refused to obey this judgment of the court. For their part the civil authorities insisted that the judicial ruling must be respected, to which the enraged Catholics responded by blocking the entrance to the cemetery. The army had to intervene so that the excommunicated Guibord was at last allowed to lie with his kin in the Montreal Catholic cemetery—but not yet for eternity.

In fact, the angry bishop decided to appeal the lower court's judgment to the Quebec Court of Appeal, which reversed the decision. And so the coffin was dug up for the second time, and poor Guibord was returned to the Protestants. And that's still not the end of the story.

As there was no Supreme Court of Canada at the time, Guibord's family and friends decided to appeal their case to the Privy Council in London. And once again, the inevitable happened. Now it was the Privy Council that reversed the decision of the Quebec Court of Appeal, and the Montreal diocese had to obey the judgment of what was then the highest court. Poor Guibord's coffin was for a third and final time pulled out of the ground and reburied in the family plot in the Catholic cemetery, this time for good and all. I've been told that the bishop put up a fence around the plot and declared that enclave was no longer part of the cemetery. That may be true, though I still can't believe it.

The church finally had to obey the courts' rulings. Bravo for the independence of the judiciary, one of the curbs on power that are absolutely crucial to the proper functioning of any self-respecting democracy. Whether we like it or not, religion has always been a player in political debate everywhere in the world. Today, in Quebec, secularism is being practised as the new religion.

10

THE ORDER OF MERIT, AND SINGING FOR THE ROYAL FAMILY

When Queen Elizabeth II graciously bestowed on me the Order of Merit in 2009, it was a surprise to many people, because I am only the fourth Canadian to receive the award since the order was founded in 1902. Two others were also prime ministers, William Lyon Mackenzie King and Lester B. Pearson (after he had received the Nobel Peace Prize); and the third was Dr. Wilder Penfield, founding director of the Montreal Neurological Institute.

The candidates are chosen by the Queen, and her citation indicated that the primary reason for her choice was my forty years of public life. It was during the celebration of Canada's centenary in 1967 that I had the privilege of meeting Her Majesty for the first time, and I am probably the Canadian public figure who has worked with her most frequently since that time.

When I was minister of Indian Affairs and Northern Development, Aline and I were tasked with accompanying the Queen, Prince Philip, Prince Charles, and Princess Anne for four days in the Northwest Territories, from Frobisher Bay (today Iqaluit) to Fort Providence, on the occasion of the Territories' centenary. Every day I travelled by plane for hours with the Queen and Prince Philip, and as the heir apparent never travels in the same plane as his mother, Aline flew in another plane with Charles and Anne.

The queen preferred speaking French most of the time, which enabled her, she said, to practise her French. Sometimes I like to say that on the contrary, it was because she couldn't stand my English!

You can imagine the joy of the Eskimos (as they were called at the time; the word Inuit has since replaced it) each time we stopped in one of their communities. We had a number of amusing experiences, and our journey to Fort Providence marked the beginning of what I call my "royal jokes."

Our stop in that Indigenous village near Yellowknife in the southwestern part of the Northwest Territories was the last of our journey, and there the Queen unveiled a monument to the memory of Alexander Mackenzie, the explorer who in 1789 discovered the great river that today bears his name. Once the event was over, the master of ceremonies had to go to the microphone to sing the national anthem, but in a fit of stage fright, he begged me to take his place. My sense of duty obliged me to agree, and it was an utter disaster! I stood up in front of three thousand people, including the Queen and the royal family, and sang the national anthem in French, because I did not then know the English words. No one in the crowd sang along, other than a few nuns from the francophone mission. As I do not have the voice of a Marc Hervieux, I was in a sweat, people were smiling, and Aline was terribly uncomfortable. What an embarrassing situation! The Queen teased me very gently, and I replied that there were not many Canadians who had the privilege of being a soloist for the royal family. She, Philip, Charles, and Anne had a good laugh; I did too, though I have to admit that my laughter was, as they say, rather forced.

In Ottawa a few months later, several of us ministers met Prince Charles. When it was my turn to shake his hand, he recognized me immediately, and when I said that I was a bit surprised by that, he replied, a smile on his lips, "How could we not recognize you? Your interpretation of 'O Canada' in the Canadian North has become part of royal folklore."

Imagine that!

11

"THE MONARCHIST FROM QUEBEC"

When I was visiting England with Aline and our daughter, France, our high commissioner in London informed us that the next day at Buckingham Palace the Queen would be receiving a group of two hundred First World War veterans who would be happy if a Canadian minister was also in attendance. Aline and France said that it was a golden opportunity to see the famous royal residence up close, so I agreed with pleasure to join the veterans for the occasion.

The next morning, there we were at Buckingham Palace. Protocol demands that the Queen first meet "a member of her Privy Council" before seeing the veterans, and so we were ushered into another room—the high commissioner, Aline, France, and myself. The Queen had been informed that she was to meet a minister, but my name had not been mentioned. Over the last eighteen months, Aline and I had had the opportunity to meet members of the royal family five times, which was a lot for French Canadians!

Suddenly a wide door opened and the Queen appeared,

accompanied by Prince Philip. Seeing me, she exclaimed, "You again!" I instantly replied, "I am the monarchist from Quebec." Coming from a province of 7 million inhabitants, to suggest that I was the only monarchist in Quebec was perhaps not very polite. But with all the grace for which she is known, Her Majesty simply smiled.

As we were on vacation, we left London for Scotland, taking the central Highland route north through majestic scenery. Then, surprise! We arrived at Balmoral, where the Queen has her summer residence. At the castle gate there were many tourists, and the royal flag was flying over the tower, indicating that the sovereign was in residence. France said, "Papa, announce yourself! Perhaps we can visit this castle too?" But I didn't want to, and we continued on our way. A few kilometres outside the castle, we stopped in a village for gas. I was on the sidewalk when someone called to me from the other side of the street. "Aren't you Chrétien from Canada?" To which I replied, "And aren't you Sir Martin Charteris, Her Majesty's private secretary?" Sir Martin then asked me, "Why don't you come and take tea with the Queen at the castle?" I said, "No, thank you, Sir Martin, we're expected elsewhere." Few of us have refused to take tea with the Queen, but I feared I would in the end be perceived as a "Royal Nut."

Prince Charles had said that I was part of royal folklore, and the Queen recounted two anecdotes from this same folklore, told to her by her parents, King George VI and the Queen Mother, about another francophone Canadian.

When they visited Montreal in 1939, the Queen Mother was seated next to the very colourful Mayor Camillien Houde at a grand banquet, and she remarked that he was not wearing the chain of office that mayors usually wear under certain circumstances. His reply: "Your Majesty, I only wear it on special occasions!"

On an earlier occasion, Camillien Houde was proceeding along Sherbrooke Street with a royal visitor, the future King Edward VIII, and the crowd was enormous. The Queen told me that the mayor informed the Prince that some of the spectators had actually come for him, the Prince of Wales. The royal family found that our colourful mayor Camillien was decidedly very funny. Didn't Montreal's ex-mayor Denis Coderre have a bit of Camillien Houde in him?

After these few anecdotes, I hope you can see that the royal family is made up of people who like to enjoy themselves, just like the rest of us!

12

IN DEFENCE OF FREE TRADE

When I first entered Canada's Parliament in 1963, the matter of commercial relations with the United States was a very hot topic in the debates. That is still true today, and it's not surprising. Even early in the last century, in 1911, Sir Wilfrid Laurier lost an election because of his position on commercial reciprocity with our southern neighbours.

Automobiles produced in Canada were expensive because of the small size of our domestic market, and those we imported were even more costly because of very high import tariffs. In 1965, after months of negotiations, the Auto Pact with the United States was finally signed. This pact was a sectoral free trade agreement in an area that was very important for both countries.

It was important for Canada to ensure that our share of jobs in this sector was proportional to our overall population. Maintaining our level of employment was the aspect of the deal that would be most scrutinized in Parliament and the press. In general, the agreement slightly favoured Canada, but the two countries both benefited, and both were satisfied. The price of cars fell slightly and consumer choice increased; the revenue the government received from excise taxes also unavoidably decreased.

Every time there were protectionist impulses on either side, the ministers of trade in each country had to find an ad hoc solution.

The debate on the possibilities of free trade with the United States had been at the heart of political battles ever since Laurier, as much for the Liberals as the Conservatives. Under Pearson, I had been in the internationalist camp of Mitchell Sharp, who at the 1966 Liberal Party conference declared himself opposed to the economic nationalism of the former finance minister, Walter Gordon.

On their side, the Progressive Conservatives held a leadership convention in 1983, following the resignation of Joe Clark. His post was up for grabs because in a vote at the biennial party convention, he had enjoyed the support of only 66.9 percent of the delegates, and he had himself set a high bar, pledging that he would not continue as leader unless he achieved 70 percent (not 50 percent plus 1). And the issue that was most hotly debated was free trade with the United States. John Crosbie, the former minister of finance, was in favour, and the one who fought most fiercely against it was, strangely enough, Brian Mulroney.

As we all know, Brian experienced his road-to-Damascus moment and became a champion of free trade with the United States, a conversion that led to the Canada–United

States Free Trade Agreement in 1990. The 1988 election was dominated by the debate on free trade. Public opinion was divided about half and half; the Progressive Conservatives were for free trade, while the opposition Liberals and New Democrats were against. Brian Mulroney had succeeded in making free trade the linchpin of the election, and in that context the Liberals lost both the historic debate and the election that hinged on it. Luckily for me, I had left politics in 1986 and was not a candidate in 1988, or I would have been in trouble. In fact, after having been one of the advocates of free trade along with Mitchell Sharp, I would have found it difficult to join the forces opposing it—all the more so in that the interests of my voters in Mauricie were aligned with the signing of such an agreement. The region included seven paper mills, the Alcan aluminum smelter, and softwood lumber operations, all of which required better access to major markets.

The issue of free trade quickly caught up with me in 1993. I was elected prime minister of Canada on October 25, 1993, and the night of my election I was informed that Bill Clinton would be phoning me early the next morning. I was at my cottage at Lac des Piles, near Shawinigan, with my family. I told my grandchildren, come to my room because I'm going to talk for the first time as prime-minister-elect to the president of the United States.

After the usual courtesies, he said he needed me because the free trade project involving Canada, Mexico, and the United States was in great difficulty in Congress. He was convinced that it would not pass unless he could count on immediate support from Canada. I told him that I needed a certain number of amendments before we could proceed. A few hours later, James Blanchard, the American ambassador in Ottawa, contacted Eddie Goldenberg, one of my most trusted colleagues, to see what we could do. Eddie put together a committee with experts from the International Trade ministry, and began discussions with Blanchard and his associates. All that, forty-eight hours after my election, and six days before my taking the oath.

Shortly afterwards, to my great surprise, I received a telephone call from Ross Perot, who had been an independent candidate in the American presidential election in 1992. He had won 21 percent of the vote and had probably caused the defeat of another Texan, George H. W. Bush. He had campaigned against free trade, and he told me that he was sure that I was the only one who could block it, and that if I did he would erect a large monument in my honour in Texas. I replied that I was not very interested in having a monument in Texas, because no Texan could vote for me in the next election.

Presidents Clinton of the United States and Salinas of Mexico had made concessions to us on water, excluding it from the agreement, and on subsidies, dumping, the environment, and working conditions. Thus, after our conversation on October 26, 1993, President Clinton was able to pass through Congress the bill on the North American Free Trade Agreement with the support of all the Republicans, half of his Democratic allies ... and me.

I'm very curious to see what President Trump will do, given his protectionist ideas and the Republican majorities in Congress and the Senate. It will also be interesting to see what the pro–free trade Republicans of 1994 will do with President Trump's protectionism. When the Trudeau government consulted me, I told them it seems obvious that since the Auto Pact has existed since 1965 and NAFTA has been functioning quite well since 1994, I think Trump will find that it's not so simple to unmake an omelette.

13

"ALTERNATIVE FACTS" OF HISTORY

In February 2017, after he was sworn in, President Trump complained that the press was not telling the truth when they reported that the crowds for his inauguration were much smaller than they had been for President Obama in 2009. Kellyanne Conway, a close adviser to the new president, came up with the expression "alternative facts" to define their view of the situation. In a sense she was right, because if you claim something ad nauseam, even if it is not true, the "alternative facts" will impose themselves over time as accepted truth, even for many historians. Such myths become almost impossible to correct; too many people have incorporated them into their own stories as undisputed factual elements.

One night I received a phone call from my grandson Olivier, who told me how embarrassed he had been by a story that was served up to him at school about an agreement between the federal government and the provinces (minus Quebec and Manitoba), in the matter of the Charter of Rights and the patriation of the Constitution—and about my presumed role in the process. Apparently he was told that I'd spent the night in the corridors of the Château Laurier, betraying Quebec. Poor Olivier had felt humiliated.

I explained to him that after six o'clock that evening I met with no one from the provincial delegations; I spoke at 11 p.m. with Garde Gardom, the minister responsible for British Columbia, and at six o'clock the following morning with Roy Romanow of Saskatchewan. I had Olivier confirm with Aline that I was home before 11 p.m. As he had to do an assignment on the subject, he wrote the version I gave him, and his learned history teacher gave him the glorious grade of zero. Alternative facts, endlessly repeated since the dramatized packaging of the "night of the long knives," are what all young people are taught in Quebec schools today. However, a documentary film called *Canada by Night* was produced in 1999 by Luc Cyr and Carl Leblanc; it exists, and it brings together the testimonies of the major players during those hours. It totally discredits the myth about that famous night. Despite the painstaking research and fact checking in the film, its limited distribution in a climate that is blind to the truth cannot compete with "alternative facts" repeated ad nauseam both before and after.

All this took place more than thirty-six years ago, and I've been saying the same thing ever since, as have all my colleagues. But no matter, the truth cannot prevail.

After that day's meeting was adjourned, Romanow, Roy McMurtry (from Ontario) and I conferred and developed a compromise plan. I thought that the federal government ought to accept the overriding clause—the controversial "notwithstanding" clause—and I told them to go out and convince the provinces. But my job was even harder: I had to convince my boss, Pierre Elliott Trudeau. After dinner I went to 24 Sussex, and attempted without success to make the case to the prime minister and the five other ministers present. Around ten o'clock, Trudeau took a phone call, and when he returned his mood had changed. He asked me a few more questions before adjourning the meeting.

The other participants left, but he kept me back and told me that he could accept my plan if we obtained the support of seven provinces, representing 50 percent of the population; in other words, the amending formula proposed by the provinces and accepted by Quebec. Trudeau, however, had always wanted Quebec and Ontario to have a right to veto. What had happened to make him suddenly accept the notwithstanding clause that in the past he had always rejected?

The phone call that he'd received was from Premier Bill Davis of Ontario, his unconditional ally from the beginning. Davis had said that he accepted the compromise I had proposed at the end of the afternoon, and that he "would abandon ship if Mr. Trudeau did not agree to it."

In fact, it was Bill Davis who broke the deadlock, but he did not get the credit, which was a pity. What broke up the group of eight provinces that had tried to derail the whole project was René Lévesque's acceptance of an idea proposed by Trudeau that very morning in an attempt to undo the stalemate: the prime minister had suggested that Quebec might hold a referendum on the patriation of the Constitution and on the inclusion of a Charter of Rights and Freedoms. The proposition would allow René Lévesque to retake the initiative against Trudeau with this referendum, and none of the other provincial politicians wanted to oppose either a charter of rights or patriation, except Manitoba premier Sterling Lyon.

Fifteen years later another referendum was held in Quebec, amid an atmosphere of the end justifying the means, and Lucien Bouchard and the other bards of separation created out of whole cloth the supposed "night of the long knives" to incite resentment. Six days after the defeat of the Yes side, the intruder who gained access to 24 Sussex by night in order to assassinate me had apparently decided to do the job with a knife. Fortunately Aline was there to save my life. Hallelujah!

Meanwhile, and sadly, the alternative facts at the origin of many unwise moves are as deeply rooted as ever. Myths really do die hard.

14

DEMOCRACY: THE WORST FORM OF GOVERNMENT, EXCEPT FOR ALL THE OTHERS

The way things are going all over the world, it's a bad time for democracy, yet since the beginning of the twentieth century, the world has made tremendous humanitarian, social, and economic progress, particularly in countries that are, or are trying to become, democratic.

Too often people forget how hard it was to get to this point, and that if we lose our democratic backbone, it's very difficult to get it back again. Obviously, democracy is far from being a perfect system. As Winston Churchill said, to make a point, "Democracy is the worst form of government, except for all the others." It took the French Revolution and two million dead to create a first version. And yet today, in many parts of the world, it's still very hard for it to put down roots.

In the course of my mandate as Canada's prime minister, I had the privilege of meeting leaders who had risked their lives for this system of governance. One night Aline and I had the immense honour of dining with Nelson Mandela and his wife, Graça Machel. There were only the four of us, and when we came in, Nelson Mandela was standing, very upright, dignified, smiling and warm—in a word, very impressive. In fact we were so impressed that we hesitated to step forward. Aline had tears in her eyes.

Imagine being alone with this hero of a people's struggle to achieve democracy in its land. Several times he had risked assassination, and he had spent more than twenty-seven years in prison for protesting against the apartheid regime and fighting for the right of black citizens to vote in his country. By his side was his wife, Graça, widow of the prime minister of Mozambique, Samora Machel, who had died under circumstances that are still murky today, when the plane bringing him home crashed.

I felt tremendous satisfaction when we made Nelson Mandela an honorary citizen of Canada in the House of Commons—by acclamation, with the exception of one innocent whose name I will generously choose to forget. What a memorable evening! Happy is the couple that has the chance to experience an evening like that.

Russia also made democratic progress when it was invited for the first time to join the G7, the grouping of the most industrialized countries, making it the G8 at the Halifax summit in 1995. To this day, when I am asked why my colleagues from the United States, France, Great Britain, Germany, Japan and Italy wanted to add Russia to the G7, I have to answer,

"Because of Boris Yeltsin . . ." All my colleagues loved this big bear of a man who wanted at any price to make Russia a true democracy. Yeltsin said that to become a member of our group would bring about change.

Meeting him, everyone first saw the exterior: the son of a peasant, built like an ox, who had lost two fingers of his left hand while handling a grenade in his youth. But what could also be seen was the man who acted so courageously in Moscow on August 19, 1991, climbing onto a tank to inspire the crowd and thwart a coup d'état that was being stirred up by nostalgic Communists. Sidelined by the new Russian government, some among them tried to overthrow the new order by entering the capital with tanks and heavy artillery to remove Gorbachev and Yeltsin from power. Yeltsin had left his office to go down into the street and climb onto the leading tank. Despite the threatening military presence, he stopped the counterrevolution cold with his extremely daring gesture. At the risk of his life, in those crucial seconds he had done more than anyone else to advance the cause of democracy and to defeat Communism in that part of Europe.

Among others I met who helped to advance democratic values in their countries was President Fidel Ramos of the Philippines. I met him at the APEC summits and on many other occasions. Ramos nearly died in his attempt to re-establish democracy in his country. The highly corrupt President Ferdinand Marcos, husband of the outrageous Imelda, had created a terrible quasi-dictatorship on those Pacific islands. Finally running out of patience, the population went into the streets and demonstrated against the Marcos regime for weeks. In this very Catholic country, even the church joined the movement in the street.

General Ramos, who was chief of staff of the armed forces, had brought together his most important subordinates, and together they had decided to join with the more than a million Filipinos in the street demanding the immediate departure of Marcos. When Ramos arrived at the city centre, which was packed with an angry crowd, he was stupefied to find that none of the other generals had followed him.

Telling me this extraordinary story, Ramos said that he'd thought he would be killed on the spot by Marcos's troops. On the contrary, his courageous gesture precipitated the events to come, and Marcos was driven from power. Ramos took the situation in hand, re-established democracy, and was a very popular president of the Philippines for the whole of his mandate.

If we want democracy to survive the very difficult period we are now experiencing, more Mandelas, Yeltsins, and Ramoses must rise up. And I am sure they will appear, because humanity has a great need for democracy!

15

THE RUSSIANS WHO MAKE ME SMILE

Today is March 21—spring at last! The fine weather is back, and I am smiling because of that—and for another reason as well. Yes, the Russians also make me smile.

When I was the minister responsible for the Canadian North, my ministerial obligations brought me into frequent contact with our neighbours to the north. From Baffin Island to the west of Yukon, the Russians are our neighbours. And so it was that for two weeks in the summer of 1971, I headed a Canadian delegation to Moscow and St. Petersburg, and then to six cities in the vast land of Siberia. I worked with the Russians during my entire career as minister and prime minister, and I could tell you some stories. Alexander Nikolaevich Yakovlev, Gorbachev's principal adviser during perestroika, had been ambassador to Canada for ten years and became a friend. Forty-six years of professional observation of our northern neighbours qualifies me to say today that if the

Russian president Vladimir Putin influenced the American election results in November 2016, what is happening today in Washington must be as sweet as candy to him.

While we Westerners, whether American, Canadian, or European, were applauding Gorbachev's revolution, which was bringing the Soviet empire to an end, for a large proportion of the Russians it was a disaster, as Vladimir Putin regularly affirms. At the first election after the fall of the Soviet Union, Boris Yeltsin completely crushed Mikhail Gorbachev's candidates, who won only 3 percent of the vote. The main reason for this humiliating rebuff was that Russians saw the dissolution of the Soviet Union as a deep humiliation.

The entire world seems surprised by the incredible popularity of Vladimir Putin in his own country, where he is supported by three out of four Russians. I am not surprised, because he has successfully reawakened the pride of the Russian people.

Life is not easy for Russians these days, because in addition to seeing the price of oil fall by more than half over the last five years, they must also deal with the economic sanctions imposed by the European Union, the United States, and Canada. On the other hand, they have greatly increased their trade with their Chinese neighbours, and their businesses have transferred their bank accounts from New York and London to Singapore, Hong Kong, and Cyprus.

Clearly, life is harder for Russian citizens today than it was five years ago, but it is still much better than the life they had during the Communist regime or during the first years under Boris Yeltsin. The Moscow of 2018 is not that of 1971.

My government was always supportive of Boris Yeltsin, and we rejoiced when he tried to establish democracy in Russia and a market economy at the same time (without much success in either case), while the Chinese concentrated only on the market economy (which has worked very well for them). Perhaps the attempt to do both, and very rapidly, was just too much, and our Western countries did not sufficiently put our shoulder to the wheel—who knows?

While I was writing this, CNN was broadcasting a one-hour show called "Putin, the Most Powerful Man in the World." After the disappearance of the Soviet Union and the suffering of the 1990s, how proud the Russians must be to make such an extraordinary return to the world stage!

When you have worked with the Russians since 1970, you know very well that they have the best ballerinas in the world, and also some very good hockey players. But we mustn't confuse the two. When their hockey players are on the ice, they're not wearing tutus. And so it's best not to charge head down into the corners of the rink in search of the puck, because things could go *boom*! Russians are Russians....

16

AN IMPROMPTU SWIM IN NORTHERN SIBERIA

During the 1966 election campaign, Prime Minister Lester B. "Mike" Pearson invited me to accompany him on a two-day trip through the riding of Algoma East, in northern Ontario. It was the beginning of the campaign; he wanted to visit a number of cities, and as there were many Franco-Ontarians living there, at each public meeting he asked me to make a brief speech that was mostly in French.

He was a Nobel Peace Prize winner, and prime minister of the country, but Mike Pearson was still an ordinary guy who liked to laugh. He told me that sometimes politics leads to unexpected circumstances, such as the day he survived, surprisingly, a vodka toast competition in Russia in 1955, when he was minister of external affairs under Louis St. Laurent. During a dinner with President Khrushchev, it became clear that he wanted to drink the Canadians under the table. In tandem with Prime Minister Bulganin, he proposed toast after toast of vodka with pepper, while keeping an eagle eye out to be sure that it was "bottoms up" every time. To the great surprise of his Russian hosts, Mr. Pearson emerged from the dinner standing on his feet, having survived eighteen of those toasts.

I had to face a similar situation in Siberia in 1971 when I was minister of Indian Affairs and Northern Development. I was leading a Canadian delegation to the Soviet Union to compare our northern development strategies. We'd had discussions with ministers in Moscow, a visit to Leningrad (as St. Petersburg was known in the Soviet era), before leaving for a one-week tour of the vast interior of Siberia—a territory bigger than the Yukon, Northwest Territories and Nunavut (all my responsibility) combined. After visiting six different regions, comparing our methods, our institutions, our progress, and our delays, I came back convinced that the Communist regime was not going to last. But it was a fascinating journey, and at one stop I had to face the same challenge my former boss Mike Pearson had accepted sixteen years earlier.

We had been working for ten days straight, and it was agreed that we would take a day off when we reached Yakutsk, in northeastern Siberia. I said I would like to do some fishing. No problem. In the morning I was taken out in a big motorboat, no other Canadians, just me. We stopped at a beach, had coffee, walked a little. There was a man waiting and I saw in the water a chain link fence that formed a kind of basin. I approached and saw six big fish in the basin. The fisherman pulled out several of them and gave them to me; a lovely photo was taken of me and the beautiful fish, each weighing three or four pounds. Then we went back to our friends. So it's true, I went fishing in Siberia. And I can guarantee that those six fish are biting still!

This unusual fishing expedition had filled up my morning, but the afternoon would turn out to be even more surprising. After I had rejoined my delegation, we boarded an excellent boat and left Yakutsk for a cruise on the Lena River. Along the way, someone warned me, "Now is when they're going to fill you with alcohol." It was very sunny, and they set up a magnificent table laden with fresh vegetables, caviar, and some beautiful bottles of vodka.

During our cruise, toast after toast was made to the friendship of two neighbours on the polar ice cap. After more than two hours of libations, to which I was unaccustomed, the vodka had asserted itself, and the Russians suggested a swimming race, four Canadians against four Russians, between our boat and another one moored about 250 metres away.

Rather tipsy, I volunteered, along with three of my compatriots. Four Russians stripped like us to their underwear. The eight competitors lined up on the edge of the boat; a Russian brought out a gun and solemnly fired off the starting signal. The four Canadians dived in, but not the four Russians, who stayed on board with all the others, nice and dry and laughing their heads off. The water in the Lena River is as cold as the Mackenzie River in the Canadian northwest. It was not only cold but, as we say in Quebec, "frette en maudit"—pretty damn cold!

But under the circumstances, the plunge into the icy river was salutary. I swallowed a large quantity of freezing cold water, which diluted my vodka. What luck! Back on dry land, my host, the prime minister of the territory, had been laid low by the unusual amount of alcohol he'd absorbed, and had to be carried away in the Russians' arms. But the river's icy water had done its work, and I was able to leave the boat on my own two feet, to applause from my companions. Canada had won—what a memorable day!

I am probably the only Canadian who can say that he went fishing and swimming on the same day in the far north of Siberia. In the course of this journey, both competitive and friendly, I think I did honour to my former boss Lester B. Pearson.

17

TRUMP AND THE RUSSIANS

I am writing these words on March 31, 2017. All day the big American television networks, like the major newspapers, are talking only of Donald Trump and his collaborators—the Russians and Putin. The question: Did Vladimir Putin in some way interfere in the presidential election of November 2016? To me the answer is clear. When the American national security contractor Edward Snowden got his hands on thousands of e-mails and spirited them away from his workplace, he was granted asylum in Russia. And the Russians would not hesitate to use these state secrets to further what they consider to be their best interests.

Every time one of those documents became public, poor Hillary Clinton went on the defensive. The newspapers treated the revelations as headline news, and candidate Trump stoked the fire, egging on the crowds at his speeches, exhorting the Russians with: "Dear friends, we are missing some of Hillary's e-mails—don't be shy, send us more! Please, don't hold back!"

And Moscow's security services were only too pleased to comply with Trump's request!

What disturbs me today is that we are falling back into a Cold War atmosphere, and this time it risks becoming even more complicated, because there could be three players. Beginning in 1950, the Cold War was essentially a conflict between the USSR and the United States. The next time, the Chinese will be involved, and they are already much more powerful than the Russians ever were.

So why not change course with the Russians? In 1955, Lester B. Pearson was the minister of external affairs, and in that capacity he became the first Western politician to be invited to visit the Soviet leaders since the beginning of the Cold War. In his memoirs Pearson describes his long discussions with Khrushchev on the subject of NATO, and surprisingly, we learn that even then, the president of the Soviet Union wanted to enter NATO. In his own words: "You must let us in, we've been knocking on the door for two years. . . ."

Of course, NATO was created because the West feared Russia's territorial ambitions. Why then did we not accept when they offered to submit, like us, to NATO's rules? Why did we choose rather to make them, literally, our perpetual enemies?

Later, when I was prime minister, NATO's member countries again began to talk of a reconciliation with the Russians. We invited them to attend the 1995 G7 summit in Halifax as participants in a de facto G8. Why did we not continue by integrating them into NATO? In Rome in April 2002, we held a special NATO summit, to which we invited the Russians, to further the possibility of a greater rapprochement and their admittance into the orbit of Western countries. And on the occasion of St. Petersburg's tercentenary in 2003, I was in a long meeting with Vladimir Putin, the German chancellor Gerhard Schroeder, and the French president Jacques Chirac; we discussed the possibility of seeing Russia become a member of the European Union. The idea of seeing Europe extended eastward was very exciting. The integration of Russia into the EU would have added a population of 175 million people and the vast resources of this immense country, the largest in the world, to the common European market; and it would have happened just as we were witnessing the ongoing and inevitable emergence of China on the world scene. For me it was an exhilarating idea.

If we had made such a move, the Russians would have been obliged to conform to our democratic rules and adopt our standards of respect for human rights, just as the Czechs, the Poles, the Baltic states, and the other former Western members of the USSR had done when they joined the EU. Europe would have gained even more power and influence because the new grouping would have created a continental association with a very competitive internal economy, and a population much greater than that of the United States. What possibilities for our Western world!

I am still astonished that I was accepted as an active participant in this discussion: I wasn't even European. My colleagues let me speak as if I were one of them.

Now there is no more G8, the Russians are sanctioned by the Western countries, and the papers talk only about their interference in the American election of November 2016.

Imagine where we would be today if we had continued on the path of reconciliation with Russia.

18

A FORGOTTEN STORY FROM 9/11

One day, during a reception in Shawinigan, one of my former voters came up to me. She had a question that she had long wanted to ask me: "When you were asked to give your permission to the military to shoot down a Korean Airlines plane en route for Vancouver, whose pilot refused to identify himself, was it very difficult to say yes?" On that fateful day of September 11, 2001, when the Twin Towers of the World Trade Center in New York collapsed, a Korean Boeing 747 with 215 passengers on board had indeed passed over Alaska and the Yukon without reporting to air traffic control. Once over British Columbia, the Korean pilot seemed to be heading for Vancouver. It was then that the military authorities called to inform me of the nature of the problem, and to ask my permission to bring down the rogue plane to avoid a massacre in the British Columbia metropolis. If the pilot did not reply to the military fighter planes and air traffic controllers within forty-five minutes, we would have to shoot the plane down, they told me.

"Madam," I answered my constituent, "there are times when the leader of a country feels very much alone. He cannot run away. He realizes that two hundred human beings, with families and responsibilities, will perhaps be dead in thirty minutes if he says yes. But if he says no, many more thousands of honest citizens in Vancouver may become victims. So I replied, 'Yes, do your duty!'"

When I put down the telephone I was in a sweat. Fifteen minutes later I learned that the pilot had entered into communication with the control tower, and that everything was back to normal. Only then could I permit myself a long sigh of relief.

In another, earlier incident, on October 25, 1999, I was in my office and was informed of a plane flying erratically over the Dakotas. It had left south Florida more than two hours before, and no control tower had been able to establish contact with the pilots. What was more, this plane had been chartered by Payne Stewart, an excellent golfer, whom I knew and liked very much. He always dressed like a Scot in knickerbockers, stockings up to his pant legs, and a tam-o'-shanter cap, all in the tartans worn by certain clans in the north of Scotland. He was colourful, very talented, and celebrated!

The plane was heading towards the city of Winnipeg, and the air traffic controllers feared that it would crash into the Manitoba capital. I was asked to give permission for the military to bring down the plane if that became necessary. With a heavy heart, I authorized the procedure. Shortly after I made my decision, I learned that the plane had crashed in

South Dakota. Reports indicated that all the passengers died in the air due to a depressurization of the cabin at the start of the flight. The plane had then wandered for several hours on automatic pilot, the pilots having lost consciousness. It would have been very painful for me if a plane carrying one of my sports heroes had been destroyed by my order.

However, the outcome of another incident on September 11, 2001, gave me great satisfaction. On that tragic day the American government authorities had ordered all the airports in the country shut down. There were at the time a dozen planes over the Atlantic, approaching the US, and they asked the Canadian authorities to allow them to divert towards Canada. Thanks to the quick response of my transport minister, David Collenette, we were able to say yes, very rapidly. I told my people that David was right. Several airports on the Atlantic coast welcomed a certain number of planes, but it was Gander that became famous. Within a few hours the city had received as many visitors as it had citizens (6,569). There were travellers from all over, speaking many languages, with all the religions and all the skin colours in the world.

On Wednesday, March 15, 2017, I found myself on Broadway with David Collenette, Prime Minister Justin Trudeau, Premier Dwight Ball of Newfoundland and Labrador, and mayors and citizens from the region of Gander, attending the premiere of the musical show *Come from Away*, which celebrates the generosity, civility, altruism, and open-mindedness of the Newfoundlanders on this dramatic occasion. Aline and I had tears in our eyes. At a time when our southern neighbours were talking about building walls, refusing to welcome people even as visitors because of their religion, and no longer accepting Syrian refugees, we were celebrating a great example of the Canadian values of tolerance, sharing, and the acceptance of diversity in a spectacle of the highest order: the miracle of Gander. And I was there with the son of my friend Pierre Elliott Trudeau, who one year earlier, as prime minister of our country, gave an example to the world by opening Canada's arms to Syrian refugees. And so I am very proud to repeat, as I have so often done in my speeches, "Vive le Canada!"

19

MINISTER OF INDIAN AFFAIRS
AND NORTHERN DEVELOPMENT

After his first victory, on June 25, 1968, Pierre Elliott Trudeau decided to make significant changes in the cabinet he had inherited from his predecessor, Lester B. Pearson, at the end of April. Accordingly, he took me out of the Department of National Revenue and we discussed a few possibilities. Finally, he invited me to take on the ministry of Indian Affairs and Northern Development. I was surprised, but I was fine with the Canadian North, with Parks Canada, and the other responsibilities associated with the former Department of the Interior. As for Indian Affairs though, as someone who had never met an Indian (the term still widely used at the time) in his life, I didn't feel at all prepared to assume those responsibilities.

The prime minister's argument was the following: "You're from rural Quebec, from a linguistic minority, and you're a politician who is very close to the electorate, and above all, precisely because you've never met an Indian, no one can claim that you're biased. Besides, I think you'll understand them better than anyone." I asked him if I could think it over. Back in my office, the reaction of my two assistants, John Rae and Jean Fournier, surprised me. They were more than enthusiastic, because they had both had summer jobs in the Canadian North. And so I accepted with much less hesitation than I would have felt just a few hours earlier. I immediately met with my predecessor, Arthur Laing, who said, his eyes filled with tears, that he was leaving this post with deep regret. This Vancouver gentleman, much older than me, gave me a lesson in tact that I've never forgotten. He remained a member of cabinet, and when he disagreed with what I was doing, he told me so one on one, while supporting me in front of my colleagues. What wisdom and inspiration in this act of solidarity!

Today, I realize that time I spent as minister of Indian Affairs and Northern Development—six years and more— was the most formative period of my political career. From the outset, Pierre Trudeau and I were very ill at ease with the reputation that our country had acquired on the international scene for our treatment of the Indigenous peoples. Often in newspapers, international debates, and at the United Nations, Canada was accused of practising a system of apartheid like that of South Africa, with its reserves, its Indian Act, and its Department of Indian Affairs. And so we decided to carry out a vast consultation over many months, in the course of which I visited Indigenous people everywhere in Canada.

From one end of the country to the other, I heard essentially the same message: "You have taken our lands; you do not respect the treaties; you have established reserves; we are second-class citizens; we have a 'Department of Indian Affairs'; you're no better than South Africa." I talked with many people for days at a time. Once, at an assembly in northern Saskatchewan, an old Indian chief told me, "Things are getting better. I am in the same room as you and I can talk to you. Twenty years ago, I travelled thirty miles in a canoe and we went to the railroad station to greet the minister. The train slowed down and on the platform of the last car stood a man waving to us. We were told that he was our minister. . . ." The Indian chiefs dressed in their traditional regalia, and spoke in their ancestral languages with, it seemed to me, great eloquence. It was all new to me, and completely fascinating.

At the end of these long consultations, we published a White Paper that landed like a bomb. The idea that foreigners, a good many Canadians, and the Indians themselves might see in the reserve system a form of apartheid was absolutely unacceptable to Prime Minister Trudeau, to me, and to the entire cabinet. And so to be consistent, we had to abolish the Indian Act and the corresponding ministry. We had to return reserve lands to the Indigenous people, and in short, give them exactly the same rights as all other Canadian citizens. When I announced these new policies to the most important chiefs, they were open-mouthed. All I was doing was accepting their traditional demands, but . . .

A few days later, in the name of all the Indians, a young, very articulate chief from Alberta, Harold Cardinal, brushed aside our White Paper, accusing us of wanting to commit cultural genocide. "What we want is not for you to change the legal system, whatever its name. We want more services, more schools, more medical services, more economic development; all that coming from the federal government alone. Equality is not what we want."

And so we retreated, but no one in the world can say that today we are imposing an apartheid system on the indigenous peoples of Canada. What we have provided is what they wanted at the time.

After this painful period, I gave new priority to Indian Affairs. When I had been in this very difficult post four years, Prime Minister Trudeau wanted to liberate me by giving me a different portfolio, but the Indians asked me to remain as their minister. When I asked them why they wanted to keep me when they were always criticizing me, they replied, "We prefer to deal with the devil we know!" So it goes.

I stayed in that job for six years, a record then in the history of this very demanding portfolio. It was an experience that helped me tremendously in all the tasks with which I was entrusted during the next twenty-nine years of my public life.

20

NATIONAL PARKS: A PROUD LEGACY

P eople often ask me what were the most important things
I accomplished in the course of my political life. Of course,
that's a very difficult question to answer when you've been in
government for forty years, as a minister, cabinet member,
and prime minister; there have been so many things that it's
hard to choose. Of course, some are well known, such as the
Iraq war, the Clarity Act for referendums, the elimination of
the budget deficit, and the freeing up of surpluses, etc. But
others, not so well known, have nevertheless given me great
satisfaction.

When I became minister of Indian Affairs and Northern
Development, I also inherited responsibility for national parks
and historical sites and monuments. During the early days of
my mandate, the president of the National Parks Association,
Alfred Frame, paid me a visit to explain in a most learned
and convincing fashion that we in Canada were not at the
top of our game, given the vastness and beauty of our country. In a single session he was able to convince me that this

was an opportunity for a very young, thirty-four-year-old minister to make his mark. At the end of our meeting, I told him that if I remained minister for five years, I would establish ten new national parks. He replied that that was not very realistic, since only four had been developed over the last forty years. I told him that I was ready to bet him five dollars that I would succeed.

Four years later, when we had succeeded in establishing ten new national parks, he sent me a cheque for five dollars along with a letter of congratulation, saying that he had never paid a gambling debt with so much real pleasure. In fact, the bet cost him nothing, because I did not cash the cheque. Instead, I placed it in the centre of a large frame, surrounded by photos of the ten new parks.

Between word and deed there can be a very long way to go. First I visited the Cape Breton Highlands National Park with the local member and minister, my friend Allan MacEachen. I was very impressed by the beauty of the site, and also by its economic impact on the region. Allan asked me, "Why not create a park in the beautiful region of La Mauricie?" I knew that there were none in Quebec. We had them everywhere in Canada, we had a decent budget, but nothing for Quebec. The directors of Parks Canada told me that they had not been able to persuade the Quebec government to cooperate. I began by planting the idea in Shawinigan, and we formed a citizens' committee designed to put pressure on provincial politicians. No minister or MPP or candidate appeared in the region without the committee cornering him, and as the project was locally very popular, the provincial government took note. One of my good friends at Laval University, Gabriel Loubier, was provincial minister of tourism, and he understood immediately that federal government investments in this sector would be beneficial for Quebec, and so he decided to help me.

During the negotiations, Loubier came to see me in Ottawa along with Marcel Masse, minister of federal–provincial relations. Loubier appeared at the prearranged time, but Marcel Masse made us wait almost an hour, which did not put us in a very good mood. When Minister Masse arrived, Loubier said to me in a loud voice, "Here is Marcel Masse, a handsome young minister, elegant, eloquent, intelligent, ambitious—and I assure you that with a bit more experience he could take my place as minister of tourism." I do not think Masse found that very funny. But that was Loubier as I'd known him at university: a very colourful character.

Marcel Masse did not want to cede a square foot of Quebec soil to the big, bad federal government. "I will not get down on my knees before the feds," he said, something no one was asking him to do. Knowing that he was very partial to separation, I replied, "If one day you achieve your separation, I will not load the park onto trucks to haul it out of Quebec."

Loubier, on the other hand, thought that he could convince the premier, Jean-Jacques Bertrand; but in the end he could not. The evening of the day the decision was taken, there was a hockey game at the Montreal Forum between the federal MPs and the provincial members from Quebec.

Loubier said to me before the game, "Masse succeeded in blocking our project this morning. Don't miss him on the ice tonight." So during the game I found myself on the ice at the same time as Masse. When he got hold of the puck, I gave him a good body check with my shoulder. Jacques Normand, a famous actor at the time, was doing the commentary at the mic, and said ironically, "The little minister's on his ass." Loubier immediately jumped onto the ice to come and congratulate me.

After a change in the government in Quebec, when the Liberals took over, I was finally able to get a hearing from the much respected Claire Kirkland-Casgrain. And now we have four national parks: La Mauricie, Forillon, Mingan Archipelago, and the Saguenay-St. Lawrence Marine Park. They are all very popular, and no Quebecker feels humiliated when visiting them.

For every park we wanted to make, there were difficult negotiations with the provincial governments, and the agreement for the Pacific Rim on the west coast of Vancouver Island was one of the hardest to achieve. We wanted to make the magnificent and unique boreal forests a special, protected place. Giant trees lined the Pacific Ocean; the site was spectacular. Victoria MP David Anderson had set up a very active citizens' committee that applied constant pressure to the provincial authorities. Their minister of tourism was in favour but had come up against the forestry minister, who wanted to keep the immense trees for the lumber industry that's so important to British Columbia. The citizens' committee had organized a large demonstration, for which a thousand people turned out—a number that greatly impressed the media. As the main speaker for the occasion, I had asked the premier Bill Bennett to meet with me a few hours before the demonstration.

Bennett was a very colourful political figure, friendly and popular. His background, like mine, was rural, and knowing that, I felt comfortable with him. He received me politely, but I was having trouble winning him over.

Finally I took my courage in both hands and said to him, "Tonight I'll be speaking to a big crowd that wants this unique site to be preserved for future generations. Shall I tell them that you're a good guy, or an S.O.B.?" He replied, "Tell them that I'm a good guy." That is how one of the most beautiful national parks in the country was born. I kept in touch with him until his death. For his funeral the family asked specifically that I represent the federal government. All's well that ends well.

What was complicated, long, and time-consuming for nine of my ten national parks, was quite easy for the Auyuittuq Park situated in eastern Baffin Island. During one of my visits to the region, we were flying low because the pilot wanted us to see the magnificent fjord running from Pangnirtung to Broughton Island. The view was superb; on each side there were very high escarpments topped with enormous glaciers. It was breathtaking, and the equal of anything to be seen in Norway. I was sitting beside Aline. She knew that I was thrilled by the experience, and she appreciated the glorious view as much as I did, and so I said, "I'm going to make this territory into a park in your honour."

Back in the office I assembled my staff, and we worked out the required perimeters for the territory. Then I consulted the minister of Northern Development, Jean Chrétien, the minister of Indian Affairs, Jean Chrétien, and finally the Parks minister, Jean Chrétien. All three agreed to establish the national park, Auyuittuq, a magnificent territory that will remain intact and protected for future generations. In making those ten parks between 1968 and 1976, we doubled the number of acres of land incorporated into Canada's park system. Later, between 1993 and 2003, with my excellent ministers of the environment, Sheila Copps and David Anderson, we created more parks, which doubled the acreage again.

In fifty or a hundred years from now, no one will remember the names of the ministers responsible for these accomplishments, but all will be grateful to them. And so when people ask me about my greatest achievements in forty years of political life, no one thinks of Parks Canada. But I think of it, and I thank Alfred Frame, president of the Canadian Association of National Parks for having challenged me during that summer of 1968. The five dollars he risked at the time turned into an investment that was immense and lasting.

21

"DO YOU EAT BEEF, CHANCELLOR?"

During my long career in politics, the job that fascinated me most was that of minister of Indian Affairs and Northern Development. In fact I am still drawn to the "Far North," the fjords of Baffin Island, and the majestic mountains of the Yukon; Inuit villages from Hudson Bay to Grise Fiord and Alert, the northernmost settlement on Ellesmere Island; the immense tundra that is probably vaster than Europe, stretching from Rankin Inlet to the Richardson mountain chain that separates the Yukon from the Northwest Territories. It so filled me with wonder that once, making a speech in Texas, I declared that I was very impressed by the state's size because it covered a twentieth of the territory of Canada's Far North.

My ministerial responsibilities granted me the privilege of making many decisions that gave me a great deal of satisfaction. Thus, we passed laws permitting education in Inuktitut and the teaching of Indigenous culture and history. Schools and hospitals were built; diamond mines, copper mines, and mines for other minerals were opened; and so on. But it is my work on democracy, in particular, that leads me to tell you the following story.

In 1968, government in the North came down to a single man: the minister—a true colonial system. The minister named the commissioner, and the budget was prepared in Ottawa. There was a council, but half its members were named by Ottawa, and in any case, the commissioner had veto power. The last non-elected member I appointed was Pierre Genest, an eminent francophone lawyer from Ontario, the first francophone to become president of the Ontario Bar, and also a good friend of mine. Pierre was a very colourful personality who loved his martini after work. Now, at the beginning of January, the council had to approve a hike in the tax on alcohol, as recommended by the bureaucrats in Ottawa.

Pierre had trouble getting to the meeting. There was a terrible storm that day, and the temperature outside was thirty below zero. Finally he arrived and took the floor, and with an eloquence much applauded by those present, he declared that the increase in the price of alcohol in Yellowknife was inhuman, that the Ottawa bureaucrats were heartless, etc. What a success that speech was! Commissioner Stu Hodgson told me about the brouhaha, and I decided to override the opposition of the bureaucrats and to make the assembly a chamber of elected members who could henceforth negotiate with my officials, even if 90 percent of the financial resources still came from the national capital. That was the end of M. Genest's mandate with the Northwest Territorial Council.

I told Pierre later that his family had made its mark on Canadian history at two different times. "The first was when Regulation 17, abolishing the French language in Ontario schools, was voted in, and your grandfather Samuel Genest was the lawyer sent to prison (he has a school named after him in Ottawa). And the other was when your revolt at the council gave birth to democracy in the Northwest Territories. Pierre, I raise my glass to the health of the Franco-Ontarian Genests."

When I became prime minister, my government passed the law that created a third northern territory, Nunavut. What a pleasure to see an immense territory, vaster than France, now ruled by an elected council necessarily made up of Inuit, because they comprised 90 percent of the population. I had seen in Bonn, in Chancellor Helmut Kohl's office, that Inuit sculptures held pride of place among the many souvenirs exhibited in that (in my opinion needlessly spacious) room. There was at the time a tremendous debate in Europe concerning the seal hunt. Kohl told me that he had received ten times as many protests regarding the seal hunt as he had for the thousands of Africans dying of hunger at the time. One thing led to another and I invited him to visit Baffin Island. When we were at Cape Dorset at the sculptors' co-operative, I asked Helmut to grant a few minutes of his time to Jack Anawak, then the federal member from the area, who later became the first commissioner of Nunavut. Jack was an Inuit who was born in an igloo. He was the real deal.

Right off, he asked the German chancellor, who was six foot five and weighed more than three hundred pounds, "Do you eat beef, Chancellor?" The reply was of course yes, and Anawak said, "Well, I eat seal! I imagine that with the skin of cows and pigs you make shoes, purses, and clothing, so why can't we sell shoes, purses, and clothing made from the skin of the seals we eat?"

Helmut Kohl was left open-mouthed. After Jack explained to him that the Inuit didn't kill the whitecoat baby seals, the chancellor became much more conciliatory and a supporter of the Far North hunters, proving that you do not need a Harvard degree to persuade even the most powerful.

Speaking of seals, perhaps I should tell you another story on the subject. I was visiting Saint-Malo in France, and the mayor of the city, who was in the midst of an electoral campaign, decided to capitalize on the presence of the Canadian prime minister to attack me because we had halted cod fishing on Newfoundland's Grand Banks, where many of his city's fishermen went every year. In reply, I told him that he should perhaps have a talk with Brigitte Bardot and tell her that she should curb her campaign against the seal hunt. I explained that the hunters, no longer able to sell their seal skins, hunted no longer, and that the overpopulation of seals, who fed on cod, had reduced their stocks to such a low level that we had to stop the fishing.

After the ceremony, a young television journalist cornered me to say, "You've said that the seals feed on cod. Are you sure of what you're saying?" "I'm not absolutely sure, Mademoiselle, because I'm not a cod, but our biologists maintain that it's so. On the other hand, I do know for certain that they don't eat beef." That was not very polite, but the mayor hadn't been polite, either. Those listening to me had to realize that even if my forefathers left France from Saint-Malo in the sixteenth century, their descendant still retained and passed on certain French traits!

That being said, there is one aspect of the region that still worries me: the sovereignty of the Arctic islands. When I was minister of Northern Development in the 1970s, the Americans sent a big ship, the *Manhattan*, through the Northwest Passage, without asking permission from our coastal authorities. The gesture angered Canadian politicians, journalists, and commentators. After talking to Prime Minister Trudeau, I went north to near Pond Inlet. On board the icebreaker *Louis S. St-Laurent*, which was not far from the *Manhattan*, I called the captain of the American ship to welcome him into Canadian waters and to tell him that I was going to pay a visit to his ship, where I hoped to see the Canadian flag flying, as is the rule when a vessel is in foreign territorial waters. I wondered what I would do if he refused to comply with my wish. I was relieved to see the Maple Leaf flying over the *Manhattan* when our helicopter landed on the ship's bridge. Today, the Americans, the Chinese, the Japanese, and many others do not recognize that the Arctic waters are Canadian, and that the natural resources beneath the ice belong to us. The problem is the same for the Russians on the other side of the polar cap.

While I approved of the Harper government's concern for the sovereignty of the Canadian North, I thought it was unwise to be so aggressive towards the Russians, because in the struggle to have our rights over the Arctic recognized, they are our main ally. To affirm their own sovereignty, they have already placed Russian flags on the seabed of their Arctic waters.

They are, de facto, our most powerful friends in the titanic battle that is in the offing. In developing our policies regarding Russia, we must take this reality into account if we want to retain control over the Arctic islands. I was very uncomfortable when, a few years ago, a Canadian minister in the Harper administration told off the Russian minister who was attending a conference of northern nations in Iqaluit. Caution and moderation are always the best policy.

22

FROM TRANS-CANADA AIRLINES TO AIR CANADA

I t's March 5, 2017, and two o'clock in London as I prepare to board a flight for Montreal. Over recent days in the British capital, I have experienced some moments of no great importance in themselves, but in my opinion, very interesting.

Arriving in the immense Heathrow Airport with my travelling companion, Bruce Hartley, we look for the name Air Canada on a huge information board. Naturally the first on the long alphabetical list is our national carrier, and I say to Bruce, "It's thanks to me that we're at the top of the list."

In 1964, when I was a brand new federal MP in the House of Commons, I proposed a private member's bill to change the name of Trans-Canada Airlines to Air Canada (AC). The initiatives of a lone member rarely become law, because we only have an hour to get it passed, and parliamentary leaders make sure that there are enough members to keep talking until the end of the hour. And so, before the second reading is over, the initiative disappears from the agenda. When I learned that my bill was going to be debated the next day, I asked certain members to indicate to their whip that they would like to have their say on the subject. With six members asking to speak, it was clear that the bill could not be adopted in the hour allotted and was going to die its good parliamentary death. And so in principle the whips' work was done. It was then that I made a strategic move by asking, first, Rémi Paul, a Conservative member, to talk for only two minutes. I did the same with Réal Caouette, leader of the Social Credit Party. A perfectly bilingual New Democrat MP from British Columbia, Bob Prittie, agreed to the same request, and I also asked two of my Liberal friends to stay seated. At five o'clock, I stood in my place to make a short five-minute speech. I said that there were already two other TCAs (Trans Caribbean Air and Trans Continental Airlines), resulting in the fact that in airports, Trans-Canada Airlines was always low on the list, mixed in with two others.

I also argued that in addition to being naturally bilingual, the name Air Canada would put us high on the alphabetical lists of the arrival and departure boards in airports around the world. Rémi Paul rose and said simply, I agree. Réal Caouette did the same, as did Bob Prittie, in impeccable French. The two Liberal friends didn't rise. All of which meant that after only fifteen minutes there were no more speakers, and the Speaker of the House had to declare that the bill's second reading had been approved. Given the rules, the third reading now had to be approved, or else no other MP's bill could appear on the agenda of the following sessions. That is how Trans-Canada Airlines (TCA) disappeared, and Air Canada (AC) was born. The next day I received a letter from Prime Minister Pearson congratulating me on my success.

As it happens, yesterday, March 4, 2017, was a special day in England and the rest of the Commonwealth. Prince Philip announced his retirement. On the same day, the Queen received the members of the Order of Merit, to which I had acceded thanks to Her Majesty, making me the fourth Canadian member since 1902. I was seated to the right of Prince Philip for lunch. I soon saw that at the age of ninety-five, he had had enough, even if he was still in excellent condition for a man of his age. Spending sixty-four years in the shadow of his wife was perhaps a bit long for someone of his character. I had met the Prince in 1967, during the celebration of our confederation's centenary. I congratulated him then on the quality of his French, saying, "Your Highness, you speak French very well for an Englishman!" He replied, "I am not English, and I was speaking French before you were born." That was the end of the conversation.

However, at this lunch fifty years later, we talked for more than an hour and a quarter—of many things, of Canada of course, of the world, of Trump, and many other topics, with much humour, somewhat neglecting his neighbour on the left, the celebrated British architect Norman Foster.

Now, as Aline could not make the trip, I was accompanied by my granddaughter Jacqueline Desmarais de Croÿ-Roeulx.

Jacqueline's husband, Hadrien de Croÿ-Roeulx, is descended from one of the oldest families of the Belgian aristocracy, which, at the height of its power at the time of Charles V in the sixteenth century, ruled over a kingdom. Their realm was within the Holy Roman Empire, which encompassed all of today's Germany and Belgium. Jacqueline said to him before leaving for London, "Hadrien, you take care of the children here in Brussels. I'm going to lunch with the Queen of England." Nonetheless, imagine my surprise to read on Jacqueline's invitation, "Her Serene Highness Princess Hadrien de Croÿ-Roeulx." I was, after all, born in Belgoville, a village whose name derives from the Belgian investors who provided the capital to build the "Belgo" paper mill, where my father earned his living for fifty years. All of which makes one smile, and flatters one's ego.

And to cap it all off, coming out of St. James's Palace after a religious service in the Queen's private chapel and an excellent lunch with Her Majesty, Prince Philip, and the other members of the Order of Merit, Jacqueline told me, with a smile at the corner of her mouth, that a member of the protocol service apologized to her because given the order of precedence established for European royalty, she was the one who should have been sitting beside Prince Philip. "Is that so!" I replied.

23

MY FRIEND YVON

On the night of Monday, May 8, 2017, I returned from Shawinigan with childhood memories flooding my mind. That day, I had attended the funeral of my childhood friend Yvon Boisvert, who like me was born in Belgoville, a tiny suburb of Shawinigan. The name "Belgoville" was born of droll political circumstances. The Belgian engineer Hubert Biermans was, at the beginning of the twentieth century, the star of economic rescue operations in his country. He was first asked to save the Belgian Congo railroad, which was in dire straits, largely due to tropical diseases that were killing Belgian workers by the hundreds. When he had finished this incredibly difficult job, he was asked to come to Quebec to put another troubled project back on its feet, this time a pulp and paper mill. He decided to stay in Canada and took over the management of the company. He became a citizen of Shawinigan, and one of his friends, Beaudry Leman, became mayor of what was then Shawinigan Falls.

M. Biermans had caught the political bug and decided to become an MP. In our region, at the time, to be chosen as a Liberal candidate almost guaranteed electoral success, but he lost out at the Liberal convention. As he was the largest employer in Shawinigan, and he did not have the support of his fellow citizens, he became angry and decided to build a town on the other side of the little river. And so Belgoville was born. But after putting up thirty houses, he calmed down and had Belgoville annexed to the village of Baie de Shawinigan. Yvon Boisvert's father was its mayor, and my father was secretary-treasurer, which created a special bond between Yvon and me.

We shared almost all our adventures, good or bad, at school or in the street or in sports. Yvon never left Belgoville. After high school he became a loyal public servant with the labour ministry. For more than thirty-five years, his daily concern was to help out workers in difficulty. He was a pianist in his free time and, with his musician friends, would get people up and dancing two or three times a week. He was also the church organist and choirmaster, and was always an active participant in every local initiative. He still lived in the house where he had raised a family of eight children, along with his loyal spouse, Réjeanne. He had three hobbies: his garden, campaigning for his friend "Ti-Jean," and rocking on a swing in front of his house.

Every evening, after his long workday, he sat in his famous swing. Everyone came to sit with him. He could be very funny. And always charming. And, as everyone said, he had very clear ideas and expressed them with conviction. He was the sort of practising Catholic rarely seen today. When the church roof collapsed, he enlisted everyone's help, including the federal program for winter works, to rebuild it. As he'd had the support of his federal MP "Ti-Jean," he invited me, with much pride, to pay a visit to his successfully completed project once the job was done. In congratulating him, I said, "Yvon, you're as red as I am, but your masterpiece, the benches, the walls, the ceiling, is all painted blue (not a single drop of red paint), and that surprises me!" "Ti-Jean," he replied, "I have committed a mortal sin, and I'll have to confess to it."

That afternoon in May, his funeral was the kind of religious service that is no longer seen. The church was full, the priest delivered an excellent short sermon, the magnificent music was sung by fifteen monks and eighteen nuns who lived in community in the parish. Yvon had helped to train this very special choir. Many heartfelt tears were shed, and two of his daughters delivered moving tributes. One of them recounted that her father never wanted to travel. He was happy at home in Belgoville, where everyone came to see him on rue Biermans; the prime minister of Canada of course, but also the presidents of France, Chile, and Israel, and the prime minister of Belgium. And so why leave his swing?

Well, yes, as when I had the pleasure of receiving at my home in Shawinigan Jacques Chirac, Ricardo Lagos, Shimon Peres, and Jean-Luc Dehaene, I showed them the working-class neighbourhood where I was born, and right beside our old house these chiefs of state greeted my friend Yvon. Even in front of them, he called me "Ti-Jean," and greeted "the lovely Aline." For everyone it was a special moment full of gratitude, respect, and love.

During the three last years of his life, he lived in a retirement home, afflicted with the terrible Alzheimer's disease. Every day he asked to go back to Belgoville. He has finally returned there forever and lies now in the cemetery he helped to maintain at the top of a hill with a beautiful view of the Saint-Maurice River.

My life has led me far from Belgoville, while Yvon Boisvert spent all of his on rue Biermans. On this sad afternoon, it was clear that you don't have to become prime minister in order to lead a useful life in one's community. All of Belgoville warmly showed that on this day.

Bravo, my friend—your life was a magnificent success!

24

SPEED, THE POLICE, AND ACADIANS

During my forty years of political life, Aline and I were obliged to manage two residences, one in Shawinigan and the other in Ottawa. We were on the road every weekend, and as political life kept us very busy and pressed for time, if we wanted to get everything done, we sometimes exceeded the speed limit. Aline made the four- to five-hour trip with the children, who found it very long. She sometimes transferred some of this pressure to the accelerator, to the point where she almost lost her driver's licence on a few occasions. But it led to some good little stories.

On the morning of August 21, 1979, I left Shawinigan for Ottawa in order to attend the funeral of former prime minister John Diefenbaker. Near Berthierville a policeman stopped me for going too fast. To avoid a fine, I told him, "Excuse me, officer, but if I'm going fast, it's because I'm late for the funeral service of John Diefenbaker, and I want to be sure that he's really dead." The policeman, who was not lacking in humour, was ready with a snappy comeback:

"Make sure it's really true!" he said, and let me go without a fine.

Another time, in the autumn of 1984, I was going from Ottawa to Lac des Piles in a new car that I was driving with special pleasure after I had lost my ministerial post and the car that came with it, following the victory of Brian Mulroney. Around Louisville, I wanted to test the maximum speed of the new vehicle. Obviously, I was going way over the speed limit, and I was pulled over by the provincial police. I handed my driver's licence to the officer, and he returned to his car. I watched him through the rear-view mirror, and I saw him laughing with his partner. I said to myself, "Oh là là! This is going to cost me plenty!" The two policemen came towards me, smirking. One of them said, "We're in negotiation with the government of M. Lévesque for the renewal of our collective agreement, and it's not going very well for us. So if you promise us to continue giving him a rough time, we'll let you go without a fine." It wasn't very hard for me to say to them that I only had to keep on being myself in order to respect their wishes. And I got back on the road with a lovely memory, and of course, without a fine.

In 1986, having left political life for a few years, I went to work for a law office in Ottawa and also for Gordon Capital in Montreal. One day I agreed to an important lunch date in the larger city, but on the way I stopped off at a school in Ottawa to give a free talk. Coming out, I saw that I had a ticket. Then I was delayed by a series of public works projects, and finally, very late, I at last got onto the highway with the accelerator pushed to the floor. A few kilometres later a policeman stopped me, and I said to him, "This is not my day; I gave a charitable speech at a school that I left with a parking fine; I was already late, and roadwork slowed me down even more, and now you're putting the icing on the cake and my lunch is toast." "Listen, M. Chrétien, I'm one of your biggest fans and it will be my pleasure to do you a favour. Follow me, and you'll be on time." He jumped into his car, switched on his flashing lights and his siren, and we took off at 140 km/h. Even though he was an Ontario policeman, he went on for some distance into Quebec territory. Then he stopped, shook my hand, and asked me to return to politics. I received no fine and he wished me good luck. He did, however, give me one little warning: "Don't tell anyone about this or I might have problems...." I arrived in time at my appointment, with a big smile. There are days like that that begin badly but end well all the same.

In 1990 I returned to politics at the head of the Liberal Party of Canada, and I became MP in the seat of Beauséjour in New Brunswick in a by-election. I stayed there for three years, and for Aline and me it was a wonderful experience to serve the Acadians and the anglophones of the region. We had the privilege of rubbing shoulders with the descendants of the Acadians, the proud people that lived through a deportation and returned to their land, courageous and as determined as ever. The Acadians now make up almost a third of the province's population. At the G8 summit in Halifax in 1995, the Acadian singer Marie-Jo Thériault performed "Évangeline" for the wives of the chiefs of state; it was the best possible way of recounting the history of her people. Extremely moved, Boris Yeltsin's wife shed copious tears.

Those francophones outside Quebec are for me inspiring people, who have succeeded in protecting their language while in a minority position. In a certain way, I find them even more admirable than Quebec francophones. One day, when Aline was driving a car a bit too fast in Acadian territory, she was stopped by the "police montée," as they are referred to there. In the language unique to the region, "Chiac," the policeman asked her for her driver's licence. Finally realizing whom he was dealing with, he then said to her, "Your name is Aline Chrétien. Are you the wife of Chrétien who I always see on TV? Well, well! You don't say . . . I'll be damned! Can I give you a warning?" There are days like that when you can't help liking the police . . . and when you're happy to be living with them and with the Acadians.

25

GENERAL DE GAULLE

Fifty years ago this year, we celebrated the centennial of Confederation, highlighted in spectacular fashion by Expo 67, the World's Fair in Montreal. Jean Drapeau's dream was a spectacular success. That summer, crowned heads and heads of state from around the globe came to Montreal in great numbers, and the most remarked-on visit was that of General de Gaulle. Of all the members of that day's federal cabinet, I am among the very last still around to speak about it.

The famous "Vive le Québec libre!" of the French president Charles de Gaulle is still being debated. Did he make his famous declaration in the heat of the moment before a huge, enthusiastic crowd at the Montreal city hall, or had he, on the contrary, planned this stunning proclamation long before? Myself, I believe that he had carefully prepared everything.

First, he came up the Saint Lawrence River on board a French ship, the *Colbert*. When the presidential boat entered Canadian territorial waters, he refused to raise the Canadian flag, as maritime protocol requires. The day before, Mme Jean

Drapeau had talked to him about his scheduled visits to Montreal and Ottawa, and he had replied that he would not be going to Ottawa as planned. He had made a triumphal journey between Quebec and Montreal. At a reception during his stop in Trois-Rivières, the mayor introduced me to him as the federal minister for the region, putting great emphasis on my youth (I was thirty-three years old) and my promising future on the federal scene. Had we been on the ice in the far north, his reaction could not have been more frigid. He was much warmer to the provincial representatives. And as we know that he prepared all his public pronouncements with great care, it's clear to me that he knew perfectly well what he was going to do three hours later in Montreal.

The next day I was at a cabinet meeting in Ottawa. Prime Minister Pearson and all the ministers were furious, the Quebec ministers even more than the others, and Léo Cadieux, the minister of national defence, told the prime minister that if De Gaulle came to Ottawa, there would be no soldier there to greet him. At the end of the meeting, Pearson informed the French president that he was no longer invited to visit the capital and that he must leave the country immediately.

Even today, it is still the biggest political controversy that I have known; a true national and international explosion of tremendous impact. Canada remained Canada, and Quebec has remained a province of Canada, and France has remained France. But what fireworks!

JEAN CHRÉTIEN

This event resulted in a few anecdotes that I am happy to share. While I was minister of Indian Affairs and Northern Development, I visited the Aboriginals in Northern Australia and the Maoris of New Zealand. During a stop in Tahiti, I met with the local authorities. At the same time, a delegation of French senators happened to be in Papeete. We found ourselves at the same reception, and a lively discussion began between the local elected officials and the Paris senators on the question of how much autonomy this Pacific territory ought to have. I took the floor and said to the mayor, "Mr. Mayor, if this can be any help to you, I can go to the city hall tomorrow and declare, 'Vive le Tahiti libre!'" Of course, not everybody found me funny. We were on a mountain among palm trees, with a magnificent view of the Pacific Ocean; all the tables were gathered around a pool filled with floating orchids. The mayor, who found himself facing me from the other side of the pool, asked me three or four times in a loud voice, "Minister, are you still coming to city hall tomorrow morning?" I would have loved to see the telegram the governor of the colony sent to the French authorities the next day....

Around the same time, I found myself in Shawinigan for the military ball of the Twenty-Second Artillery Regiment. The guest of honour was the French ambassador Pierre Siraud, and the ball was hosted by Colonel Gérard Dufresne, a businessman in the city. The mayor had held a reception for the ambassador and Monsieur Dufresne. At a certain moment, the mayor invited the ambassador to take the floor.

Like a very good Frenchman, he expressed himself with great elegance and spoke of Quebec and Quebeckers, of France and the French, but forgot Canada and the Canadians. Colonel Gérard Dufresne was known not to mince his words, especially when he had taken a glass. He and his wife were members of two old and very respected families. Their fathers were a doctor and a pharmacist. Madeleine was particularly well educated, and a bit more bourgeois than average. She wanted her husband, as a good host for the evening, to behave himself and made him promise not to drink that night. But for Gérard, that was asking a lot.

At the end of his speech, the ambassador came to greet me and said, "I understand that you will soon be coming to France, Monsieur le ministre, and if I could help you, I would be very happy." I replied: "You are very kind, Monsieur l'ambassadeur, but I suggest we talk again when we are back in our other country in Ottawa." Immediately, Dufresne gave me a tap on the shoulder and said, "You know, you're quite a guy. . . . Come and have a drink. . . ."

Two or three glasses of Scotch later, when Gérard was sitting across from the ambassador at dinner, he became very talkative. It was a long dinner for Madeleine and the guest of honour. In colourful language, very direct and seasoned with spicy epithets, the ambassador was informed that most Quebec nationalists of the time had opposed the war effort, that they had enthusiastically supported Pétain, and they had hidden collaborators in their houses and convents, while he, Gérard Dufresne, was lowering into the ground some of his comrades who had fought in France and Holland, where he had been wounded, etc. When the time came for the ambassador to thank his host, he found at least five opportunities to use the words "Canada" and "Canadians."

Then Gérard became the perfect host; he elegantly introduced the ambassador to everyone and invited him to dance with "supremely elegant" women, who would be very happy to waltz with a personage as important as the guest of honour, the French ambassador. If the dinner had been rather awkward, the ball turned out to be perfect.

At the moment of parting, Gérard asked his guest if he sometimes talked to his president, General de Gaulle. The ambassador said yes, he did. "Well, tell him that he has a great admirer in the person of Colonel Dufresne, who fought by his side to free the mother country, and that the next time he comes to Canada, he should mind his own business." I am sure that dear M. Siraud never forgot that evening with the federalist soldiers of Shawinigan.

During the Sommet de la Francophonie in Bénin in November 1995, shortly after the Quebec referendum that the No camp had won with a very slim majority, President Chirac said a few things that displeased me.

Shortly after his speech, Chirac received me for a bilateral meeting between the two countries that were the pillars of the francophone world. In the course of the meeting, I told him quite clearly that his remarks during his speech and during the referendum had not been appreciated. I also reminded him that if we French Canadians still adhered to the French language and culture, it was thanks to Canada. Because unlike the francophones of Louisiana and New England, we had prospered in Canada while the French language and culture had to all intents and purposes disappeared from Louisiana and the northeastern states of the United States. I informed him that my father, Wellie Chrétien, who spent the first ten years of his life in Manchester, New Hampshire, kept his language and culture when he came to Quebec, whereas his cousins in the United States had changed the family name to Christian. To finish my tirade, I stood and raised my arms to the sky like General de Gaulle, saying to President Chirac that he would certainly not like it if I were to go to France to declare, "Vive la Corse libre."

The French and Canadian officials were very surprised, if not shocked, by this unusual outburst, especially Jean Pelletier, my chief of staff, and a great friend of Chirac's. Later Pelletier told me that my frank talk had impressed the French president and that I had gained his respect. We later became good friends; he came to the Sommet de la Francophonie in Moncton in 1999 and had a memorable visit, along with his wife, Bernadette, Aline, and myself, with the Inuit on Baffin Island. Two days before I left my post as prime minister in December 2003, he hosted a magnificent dinner in my honour in the presence of the prime minister, the minister of Foreign Affairs, and the crème de la crème of French society. In his speech on that occasion, with all the eloquence of which he was capable, Jacques Chirac praised the political, economic, and social life of our country, and concluded by lifting his glass and proclaiming, "Vive la France, vive le Canada!" We were now a long way from the famous words uttered on that balcony at Montreal city hall in 1967.

26

RELIGION AND POLITICS: AN AGE-OLD DEBATE

It was a simple municipal resolution aimed primarily at Muslims and Jews (without mentioning them specifically), passed by the aldermen of St-Timothée d'Hérouxville, that triggered the debate on Quebec values that continues to traumatize our province many years later. But at the time, no member of either of those communities lived in this village situated not far from my hometown. When I think about it, I fall back on the expression popular in the region: "J'ai mon voyage!" Loosely translated, it means "I've had it up to here!"

To be an alderman in Hérouxville is not a full-time job. The alderman who launched the psychodrama had lived for a while in the Middle East and probably just wanted to amuse himself when he proposed the fateful resolution that made him an overnight international celebrity. And it gave rise to, among other things, the Bouchard-Taylor Commission and the minister Bernard Drainville's Quebec Charter of Values.

This largely contributed to the defeat of the Marois government at the hands of Philippe Couillard's Liberals. Today Quebec's new religion is secularism. An old crucifix in the National Assembly: a scandal! A prayer before the Chicoutimi town council meeting: a huge trial! What a waste of time and energy. But those political debates go back a long way.

At the time of Lent at the beginning of the twentieth century, my grandfather François Chrétien and his friend Dr. Milette were refused communion because during the election they had passed out alcohol to encourage the citizens to vote Liberal. Now, at the time, given the Catholic Church's canon law, it was up to the bishop to impose the sanction for such a sin. As Dr. Milette and Mayor Chrétien did not find it sufficiently important to confess to the bishop, they were the only two members of the community to be denied communion during Lent, and that before the eyes of the entire parish.

Every night my grandmother had the family pray for the conversion of the stubborn François. Easter arrived, and neither the mayor nor the doctor had observed the rites surrounding this sacred celebration. What a scandal! The two of them were surely going to Hell. During the week following Easter Sunday, however, it was still possible to redeem oneself. In fact, the Bishop of Trois-Rivières had dispatched a Franciscan father to Saint-Étienne-des-Grès to confess Chrétien and Milette. That done, they were both able to receive communion on Low Sunday, to the great relief of the priest and the entire community. Like the rest of the parish, they could now go to Heaven. When my father told me this story, he said, with pride, "It was the bishop who gave in." Fulfilling one's Easter obligations on Low Sunday was called "the fox's Easter." They had taken everyone by surprise.

Fernand D. Lavergne was an influential union man from Shawinigan. He was president of the Cooperative Commonwealth Federation (CCF) in Quebec—the precursor of the New Democratic Party (NDP)—and in the federal election of 1958, Lavergne was the CCF candidate. Two of his children had to go down on their knees with the other students, on the order of the teaching sister, to pray that the "Communists" (the CCF) would not be elected in our riding. They had to pray for their father to lose the election. They went back home with tears in their eyes and told their father, who was a practising Catholic.

Furious, Fernand D. went to the Bishop of Trois-Rivières to ask for an audience with Msgr. Pelletier, a Conservative bishop if ever there was one. As you would expect, the conversation was contentious. Each held to his position, and Fernand D. said to the bishop, to end the meeting, "Monseigneur, there are only two things left that I can do. As a Catholic, I can kneel and ask for your blessing, or as a citizen I can give you one in the eye." It's said that the bishop did not go to the hospital.

Aline and I are practising Catholics, but even I have had problems with my church. During a vote in the House of

Commons, I supported the right of women to be in control of their own bodies; in other words, I voted in favour of abortion. Very close to our house there was a Catholic private school where thirty sisters lived. I had been their student for five years, and they usually voted for me, at the same polling station as we did. That year, I received twenty-eight fewer votes than I had in the last election—apparently two of them disobeyed the bishop. His involvement did not hurt me—I still easily won the election.

My difficulties continued after I was elected prime minister. My bishop in Ottawa wrote me a personal and confidential letter reminding me of my religious duties, and surprise, surprise, he published it on his website. The Bishop of Calgary got into the act to declare that I was going to Hell because I did not want to ban abortion and I allowed gay marriage in Canada. When I told Aline, she replied, "I'll go with you. We haven't been married for forty-five years for nothing." We are both practising believers because we have made Pascal's wager: if it's true, we are on the right road, and if it is not, we have nothing to lose. Why run the risk?

At any rate, in a country as ethnically and culturally diverse as Canada, where many religions are practised, I have always felt that it was politically inappropriate to want to impose one's own moral and religious values on the entire population.

27

WHY I'M A FRANCOPHONE FEDERALIST

I have often been asked how someone like me—born in rural Quebec, growing up unilingual, a graduate of Laval University in Quebec, and practising law in French only—could be such a convinced Canadian federalist. I like to answer that it's because of my family history.

My father was a devout Catholic and francophone, but his French heritage was not just Québécois. He had lived in Manchester, New Hampshire, from 1888 to 1898, and some of his family members stayed on in New England. Moreover, for fifty years he was the director of a mutual insurance company whose members had to be French-speaking and of the Catholic religion. Most of them were Franco-Americans, and Papa was one of the three directors who represented French Canadians. And so he witnessed the decline of the French language in New England, despite the heroic efforts of groups such as the Association Canado-Américain. As the American state had no interest in preserving minority languages, responsibility for preserving the French language fell to the Catholic Church, which fulfilled this task well until after the war. The author of the landmark book *On the Road,* and the most famous icon of the beat generation, Jack Kerouac, was a francophone born and brought up in the French-speaking town of Lowell, Massachusetts.

Papa told me one day that the Knights of Columbus were in large part responsible for the loss of French schools, because they lobbied Rome to always have Irishmen as bishops. Those bishops forced the amalgamation of the French and English Catholic schools, which led to the gradual disappearance of the French language in schools.

Here in Canada, he said, our constitution allowed us to keep our schools. He told us that if we still spoke French, it was because we were Canadians. If we had lived in the States, that would not have been the case. On the other hand, my mother's story is very Canadian. In 1907 my father married my mother in the Baie-de-Shawinigan church. My mother was only sixteen years old when she got married, a decision that she'd taken in part to avoid following her family to the West. And so love kept her in Quebec.

The whole family boarded a train the day after the wedding. Father, mother, children, and the newlyweds made the trip to Pembroke, Ontario, where Papa and Maman left the family caravan to continue their wedding trip. They spent their honeymoon at a hotel in a very pretty spot on the Ottawa River near Chapeau, a village later annexed to the municipality of

L'Isle-aux-Allumettes. I visited the region a few years ago and learned that the hotel had burned down just the previous year after more than 110 years of existence.

My mother's father, Philippe Boisvert, along with the rest of the family, continued the journey to northern Alberta and a parish called Thérien near the town of Saint-Paul, then called Saint-Paul-des-Métis. The Catholic Church then encouraged the growth of the Catholic, French-speaking population. We still refer to this era as that of "the revenge of the cradle." And as there was a population surplus in Quebec, many opted for the "colonization" of the Canadian West. Wilfrid Laurier's federal government had a very aggressive policy of opening up the Prairies, and many Québécois settled there in the vast open land at the same time as thousands of immigrants were arriving largely from Ukraine, Poland, Hungary, and Germany. In time, the six brothers and sisters put down roots with their families in many parts of Alberta and Saskatchewan. Maman got news of each of them by mail and liked to keep us up to date on what was happening with the Boisverts in the West. As I lived in the city, I knew a lot more about agriculture on the Prairies than in the East. One of my uncles had bought a "combine" and the other "half a section" of land, terms that became more familiar to me than the *arpents* closer to home. The French language gradually disappeared for those who left their francophone village for the city, where there was no French school.

An interesting autobiography was written by one of my cousins, Rolland Boisvert, who was honoured as the top volunteer of the previous fifty years for his involvement in his community in the Edmonton suburb Sherwood Park. This book is full of anecdotes, and one in particular shows clearly the difficulty of being francophone at that time in the West. His father and his uncle had settled in Marengo, Saskatchewan. He and his cousin turned up at the school, but their teacher refused to allow them to attend class, telling them to come back when they could speak English. So the two cousins were sent out to the schoolyard on the teacher's orders. Two francophones alone in the schoolyard: that wasn't how they were going to learn English. As they had nothing to do, they amused themselves by throwing stones. At one point one of the stones went over the school's roof and hit the principal, who happened to be outside. He finally decided that it was less dangerous to have the two Boisverts at a school desk and insisted that the teacher accept them. Despite everything, the community kept their language pretty successfully for a hundred years.

Because of them, when I was the minister responsible for the Charter of Rights, I made it my mission to inscribe in it the right to education in one of the two official languages for all citizens anywhere in Canada, and I succeeded. Marie Boisvert of Edmonton told me recently that her two daughters taught French in immersion classes, one in Alberta, the other in British Columbia. That was 110 years after the Boisverts left Quebec for Alberta. The fate of the French language, whether in New England or Alberta and elsewhere in Canada, is in my genes. For me, I am still francophone because I am Canadian. So there!

28

IN THE FOOTSTEPS OF MY GRANDFATHER FRANÇOIS CHRÉTIEN

My grandfather François Chrétien was mayor of Saint-Étienne-des-Grès for more than sixteen years, first from 1907 to 1910, and then between 1914 and 1927. He was also one of the chief Liberal organizers in the Saint-Maurice valley for even longer. And so my father, Wellie, found himself involved in political debate at a very young age. He was a great admirer of Sir Wilfrid Laurier, and one of his fondest youthful memories was of having the privilege of meeting the great man in Trois-Rivières. Inevitably, having settled in Baie de Shawinigan, he became a Liberal Party supporter, and for forty years he was its principal organizer in this parish of some 1,500 inhabitants. He liked to tell me that his parish had voted Liberal at every federal and provincial election during that whole long period. One of his ambitions was to bring up one of his children to be a politician, and when I was still very young, he decided that I had the energy and the talent required to fulfil that task.

At the age of thirteen, I became his political protegé. I helped him to distribute electoral pamphlets, I put up candidates' photographs on telephone poles, I listened to political discussions with the townspeople. In short, he trained me the way a father trains a son to become a hockey player. After my classical schooling, when it came time for me to choose a profession, I told him that I wanted to become an architect, to which he replied that I would never get elected as an architect, and that instead I would have to enrol in the law faculty. Back then, when Papa said something, you listened and that was that.

And so I became a lawyer, and then a politician. When Papa died in 1980, his protegé had been an MP for seventeen years, and a minister for thirteen years, and he was very proud of his accomplishments.

During the 1962 election, to everyone's surprise, Réal Caouette's Créditiste party swept rural Quebec, and our MP, the respected mayor J.A. Richard, who was now elderly, was swept away by the tidal wave, after serving in the House of Commons for thirteen years.

Réal Caouette was a genuine phenomenon. A garage owner from Rouyn-Noranda, he rallied to the Social Credit party, which had MPs from Western Canada in the House of Commons. This was a right-wing political party, agricultural and populist, that had emerged in Alberta before the war. Réal, as he was always known, was a superb orator, very colourful, with an amazing sway over crowds. A country's national assets were at that time largely determined by the gold reserves the state possessed. Caouette argued eloquently that the economic problems of the working class were due to the fact that the Bank of Canada did not print enough money, and that if the government ordered them to put more "piastres" in circulation, and distributed them to its potential electors, they would visit the stores and would thus turn the economic wheel and so on. All that accompanied by very funny sarcastic remarks targeting the affluent class. Obviously, that tempting populist cocktail was enthusiastically applauded as he travelled through the province of Quebec.

In 1958, at the time of John Diefenbaker's tremendous victory, Quebec elected more than fifty Conservatives. That had not happened since Laurier, and it stunned the Liberals. But the surprise was even greater when Réal Caouette's Créditistes elected twenty-six members in the 1962 general election. This conquest of Quebec by Réal Caouette meant that the Conservatives now presided over a minority government, a prelude to their defeat in 1963. The election was called in February for April 8, and as I was a young lawyer and very involved in politics since my university days, this was a terrific opportunity for me to launch my career. It would not be an easy task, since the Créditistes had won the riding with a 10,000-vote majority only nine months earlier. The Liberal Party's morale had been at rock bottom ever since the crushing defeat of J.A. Richard, and very few people thought that I would take back the seat on my first try, with many saying that I should prepare myself for the next round.

The group of young people who had joined me were determined to win, but the scepticism was so widespread that we had to do something special. One of my good friends, Guy Suzor, put together a team of ten people who went into public places such as taverns to bet five dollars on a Chrétien victory. Many Créditiste sympathizers didn't have the five dollars to take the challenge, leaving the impression that young Chrétien was gaining ground. Now, it was my brother Maurice, a well-off surgeon, who came up with the money for my friend Suzor to further his campaign.

Unexpectedly, a businessman and frequent gambler—who supported me but didn't think I had a chance of winning—accepted the challenge and deposited five thousand dollars in the Bank of Montreal. My father, three of my brothers, and I collected this sum, impressive for the time, and covered the bet within twenty-four hours. Soon word went around the city of Shawinigan to the effect that the wager had been accepted very quickly. All this activity created a sense of change, and it began to be said that the Liberal candidate Jean Chrétien was going to win, which is what happened on April 8, 1963. My brother Maurice had risked more than eight thousand dollars, and won.

After that he contributed generously to my electoral campaigns. Thirty-five years later, when he was still committing the maximum permitted by law, Aline told him that at the age of ninety he no longer had to. He replied that his contribution in fact just represented the interest on the capital he'd won in 1963.

Almost every day we had meetings in the riding's forty villages and four towns. At the time, political meetings were very popular and every candidate had to have good orators on his team to influence the voters who were present. Among those on my side, the star was always Fernand D. Lavergne. He'd been born in the same parish as me, and he was the most prominent workers' leader in the region. In 1958 he had been a candidate for the CCF and also their main spokesperson in Quebec. When I became a Liberal candidate, he joined my team. Given the respect he was accorded among the unionized workers in the region, he was an invaluable acquisition.

He talked with a fairly strong stutter, which he used with great effectiveness. His sense of humour was unbeatable. Here's an example: Créditiste MP Gérald Lamy argued in his speeches that at the age of twenty-nine I was too young to be elected. In reply, Fernand D. delivered the following tirade: "M. Lamy, the Créditiste MP, wants you to vote for him because he has fifteen children; M. Pellerin, the Conservative candidate, wants you to vote for him because he has fourteen. I'm not running this time because I have only eight. M. Lamy deserves a lot of credit for having fifteen children, but if he's like us, he must have had some fun along the way. Jean is only twenty-nine years old, and we Catholics have a right to just one wife. If he were obliged to have fifteen children, that might raise certain questions." With his controlled stutter, what followed went something like this: "What it comes down to, ladies and gentlemen, is that we are looking for a 'rrrrrrrrrepresentative,' and not a 'rrrrrrrrrreproducer!'" Imagine the effect of that tirade!

Fernand D. was twenty years older than me, and had a long and rich experience in life. In his wisdom, he gave me the best advice I've ever had: "In everything you do in public life, have confidence in the judgment of the people." During my entire political life, I've kept that in mind. Thank you, Fernand!

29

LIFE AFTER POLITICS

What happens when you wake up one day and you're no longer the head of government? Mike Pearson said that he didn't know how to make a telephone call. Bob Rae, former premier of Ontario, has said that he sat in the back of his car before remembering that he no longer had a chauffeur.

As for me, two days after my retirement from political life, I went to Montreal with Aline. I still had a government car and the driver, an RCMP officer, let me off where I had my appointment. Then I asked him to drive Aline to Sherbrooke Street. He dropped her off in front of a store, where she asked him to wait. When she came out, the car wasn't there. The weather was bad, and more than twenty centimetres of snow had accumulated on the ground. There were no longer any telephone booths on the street, and she was the last customer in the store, which was now closed. Helpless, she asked a passerby if he could lend her his cellphone so she could call me. I told her to wait, and I reached the officer to ask him why he had not been there for Aline. He said that his superior had told him that Madame no longer had a right to chauffeur services. When I arrived thirty-five minutes later, Aline was on the sidewalk in the middle of a snowstorm, without boots, chilled to the bone. She had been the wife of the ex–prime minister of Canada for thirty-six hours. The transition was brutal.

Aside from that incident our return to private life was very easy. I became a legal counsel in a large law office. My income was far superior to the salary of a prime minister, who, in fact, earns less than the worst hockey player in the NHL. I made well-paid speeches in Canada, the United States, Europe, and even in Africa. Aline adored this new, calmer life, and liked to say that she had been the wife of a politician for forty years and yet she was still smiling. Both of us became involved in volunteer activities. Aline was chancellor of Laurentian University in Sudbury. I teased her, saying that in going to university for the first time in her life, she had might as well start at the top as chancellor. We were co-presidents of the largest fundraising effort for the University of Quebec in Trois-Riviéres. We agreed to dis-creetly do work for all sorts of charitable organizations. Prime Minister Harper had promised at a Commonwealth meeting to do something special to celebrate the sixtieth anniversary of the coronation of Queen Elizabeth II, and he asked me to represent Canada on the committee presided over by John Major, former prime minister of Great Britain. Canada contributed to the program proposed by Major, but at the suggestion of Governor General David Johnston, I undertook a strictly Canadian project, the program of Jubilee grants. I asked for the help of many of my former colleagues, premiers of the provinces, and with the help of my two assistants, Bruce Hartley and the ambassador Patrick Parisot, we persuaded the federal government, the provinces, the private sector, university foundations, and others, to contribute. It is all now managed by the Governor General's Rideau Hall Foundation. We raised almost eighty million dollars. Now, hundreds of Canadian and foreign students are benefiting from the Jubilee grants. I want to emphasize the special efforts made by former premiers Brian Tobin, Frank McKenna, John Hamm, Roy Romanow, and Gordon Campbell. At the beginning, I had been unhappy to have my arm twisted by Stephen Harper, who told me that since I was the only Canadian to have been admitted to the Queen's Order of Merit in fifty years, I ought to accept. Now I'm very happy to have taken the challenge. All's well that ends well.

Thirty-three years ago, a group of former heads of state and/ or government formed an association called the InterAction Council. Among the founders besides Pierre Elliott Trudeau were the former German chancellor Helmut Schmidt, the former French president Valéry Giscard d'Estaing, the former prime ministers James Callaghan of Great Britain, Yasuo Fukuda of Japan, and Malcolm Fraser of Australia. Every year, twenty or more men and women, all former heads of government, meet in a different country to discuss with experts (all voluntarily contributing their time) the social and political situation around the world. This year, for example, we discussed health, water, the environment, and the impact of Trump. We were in Ireland, in the charming city of Dublin.

For a long time the de facto president of the InterAction Council was the impressive intellectual who had abandoned writing to practise politics and then returned to writing and teaching, the unique Helmut Schmidt. In fact, he was the guiding light for thirty years, until his retirement at the age of ninety-four for reasons of health. When I became a member of the council in 2004, Helmut Schmidt was co-president along with Malcolm Fraser, the former prime minister of Australia. In 2007 I became the co-president, and in 2008, Franz Vranitzky, who had been chancellor of Austria, became my co-president.

The nine years spent at the head of this organization were very stimulating. Preparing the program, holding preliminary meetings with experts from different countries, finding the funds for the group, was both demanding and satisfying. I left the presidency in 2016, and the InterAction Council completed its thirty-fourth meeting in 2017 with co-presidents Bertie Ahern, former prime minister of Ireland, and Olusegun Obasanjo, former president of Nigeria, at its head. My friend Tom Axworthy, former principal secretary to Pierre Trudeau, a most dedicated volunteer and prolific contributor, managed the organization out of Toronto with the help of the excellent Tanya Guy, a boon for Canada and a loss to Japan.

During lunch one day, Bernadette and Jacques Chirac talked to us of a museum they had built in the commune in

Corrèze where Bernadette was mayor, to display the gifts they had received during their very long public lives. After visiting this magnificent site with its stunning architecture and beautiful surroundings, all in the best French tradition, Aline and I decided to follow suit. As I like to say, "For Aline, eight hundred presents in the living room would collect way too much dust." And so we put all our presents at the disposal of the Cité de l'Énergie, a non-profit theme park, with a science centre and a historical sector, in my hometown of Shawinigan. Under the guidance of the amazing Robert Trudel, thousands of people come every year to visit the Prime Minister Jean Chrétien Museum, whose theme is "Canada in the World." It's all well done, and those who go there emerge surprised, informed, and very satisfied.

As I write these lines I'm in a plane over the Atlantic, and I'm thinking of the thirteen years since my retirement from political life. I have just passed the baton of the InterAction Council presidency, and I'm on my way back to Canada. In a few days, Aline and I will leave the life we love in Ottawa to spend the summer at home at the magnificent Lac des Piles in Mauricie, surrounded by the fellow citizens who enabled me to have this long, beautiful forty-year career in public life. What is more, I am returning to my three children, my five grandchildren, and my six great-grandchildren, among whom is William, whom I accompanied this winter on his first run down a ski slope. But most important, I'm returning to Aline, the love of my life for sixty-five years, sixty as my wife, my eternal Rock of Gibraltar. Dear God, what more could I ask?

30

AN INSPIRING TRIP TO EUROPE

It's Sunday, July 2, 2017. I'm just back from a short trip to Europe, where we celebrated July 1 along with seven hundred guests at our magnificent Paris embassy. It felt strange to be marking Canada's 150th anniversary in the land of my ancestors, who in 1660 left the town of Loches in the département of Indre-et-Loire. Our ambassador, Lawrence Cannon, and the number two at the embassy were very welcoming. Especially the latter, Graham Clark, who, after I borrowed him from the Department of Foreign Affairs, was my legislative assistant for two years. He's the son of a very distinguished public service family in Ottawa.

The French journalists were very eager to talk to me about our prime minister, Justin Trudeau, and to compare him to President Macron. They had just as much to say on the subject of President Trump, and were very happy that a modern and progressive politician is leading Canada at this time. They were intrigued to learn that before the reception I had gone to see Jacques and Bernadette Chirac. I had to acknowledge that the former president's health was fragile, but when I told them that he had asked me to embrace "the lovely Aline," one of them said, "Good old Chirac!"

During my European tour I took the high-speed train, the TGV, which covers the distance of five hundred kilometres between Paris and Strasbourg in less than two hours. The TGV makes this trip six times a day, connecting Paris to a city of 400,000 inhabitants. On my way I asked myself why I had not done the same thing for Quebec City's 800,000 inhabitants and Montreal's 3 million, Ottawa's 1,200,000, Toronto's 7 million, London's 350,000, and Windsor's 210,000?

In fact, I'd appointed Jean Pelletier to launch just such a project, but we ran out of time. It's too bad, because since I retired almost fourteen years ago, nothing at all has been done.

I went to Strasbourg to attend the funeral of former Chancellor Helmut Kohl. I was not sorry to make the long trip because I was able to meet Chancellor Angela Merkel for the first time and to congratulate President Macron. The tribute to Chancellor Kohl took place in the magnificent European Parliament in Strasbourg, and I had the opportunity to talk with many people I had known who were leading, or had led, their countries, such as Dmitri Medvedev, prime minister of Russia, Martin Schulz, Merkel's rival during the September 2017 election, Theresa May of Great Britain, presidents Clinton and Sarkozy, and prime ministers Berlusconi and Prodi of Italy, John Major of Great Britain, and José María Aznar of Spain.

It was gratifying to hear the congratulations for Canada, Trudeau, our generosity in welcoming refugees, and the example we had set. The former president of Slovakia, Rudolf Schuster, who had lived in Canada, simply said, "Canada, the best country in the world," a statement I have often heard. And Sarkozy introduced me as someone who had saved modern Canada—an exaggeration, no doubt, but magnanimous.

But what was most important was to see all these European leaders paying tribute to a politician who had believed more than any other in building Europe—who had rapidly unified Germany; who had to all intents and purposes created the common currency, the euro; and who had established his country as the pre-eminent power in Europe. He was also the only one among us who had lived through bombing, and he believed that a united Europe was a necessary bulwark to ensure that the continent never again had to experience the horrors of war.

Seeing Macron, Merkel, and Prime Minister May, I wondered what had finally prompted the British to abandon Europe. One of the explanations seemed to be that they had never decided to be European and therefore to fully assume their role in Europe. President Charles de Gaulle was never enthusiastic at seeing the English in the European Community because he must have feared their possible domination of the European Union.

On the other hand, British politicians were afraid of losing their identity. They had lost their global supremacy with the collapse of their empire, and instead of taking full advantage of their membership in the future European federation, they always insisted on making an exception of themselves, for example by keeping the pound and not buying into the new European currency, the euro. In time they were marginalized, and the English, French, and German trio was replaced by the French-German duo. Rather than being half-European in an E.U. role that was increasingly peripheral, the proud English simply preferred to leave. At the tribute to Chancellor Kohl, Merkel and Macron were the centre of attention, and Prime Minister May seemed not to exist. I think that's too bad.

That is why I always thought that Quebec should play its full role in the Canadian federation and not risk marginalizing itself as the British are doing in Europe. Prime Minister Lester B. Pearson understood well that for Canada to be effective there had to be a strong representation from Quebec. In the beginning he recruited two disciples of one of the pioneers of the Quiet Revolution, Father Georges-Henri Lévesque at Laval University: Maurice Lamontagne and René Tremblay, along with the deputy minister of justice, Guy Favreau. As if that were not enough, in 1965 he invited three very prominent Québécois to join his team: Jean Marchand, Quebec's most important union leader; Gérard Pelletier, the chief editorial writer of *La Presse*; and the controversial intellectual Pierre Elliott Trudeau. Once he became prime minister, Trudeau followed the same path, and he was so successful that throughout his time as head of government, political observers in English Canada would talk, not always in a friendly way, about "French power."

When my turn came, I was determined to continue in the same direction. This was rather difficult, because as we were preparing for the 1993 election, the country was deep in a constitutional debate in the aftermath of the collapse of the Meech Lake Agreement. Nevertheless, I was able to attract two very influential deputy ministers to Ottawa, Marcel Masse and Michel Dupuis. But my greatest successes were within the administration. At one point, francophones in positions of power included Governor General Roméo Leblanc; chief justice of the Supreme Court Antonio Lamer; chief of the Canadian Armed Forces Maurice Baril; the Clerk of the Privy Council, and thus the senior officer in the federal public service, Mme Jocelyne Bourgon; our ambassador to Washington Raymond Chrétien; the exceptional Jean Pelletier, former mayor of Quebec City, who was my chief of staff; and myself, of course, as prime minister. A little later in my administration, five of the nine judges on the Supreme Court were francophones, when the excellent legal minds Michel Bastrache and Louise Arbour, representing respectively the Maritimes and Ontario, joined the court. And Gilbert Parent was Speaker of the House of Commons.

I was very satisfied with my performance in that area, but what gave me the greatest pleasure was that during that period there were no hostile articles published, in contrast with the time of Trudeau. What seems clear is that no one cast any doubt on the competence of any of the persons referred to above. As a result, the years 1993 to 2004 marked the high point for the French language in the federal administration.

From that I draw two main conclusions: when we are in a minority but claim our place through hard work and competence, no obstacle is insurmountable. And as for the separatist claim that francophones are always scorned or sidelined, it was clearly contradicted by their massive presence in the federal administration at the turn of the millennium. There is no doubt that when we give of our best, nothing is beyond us.

To return to my visit to the Franco-German frontier: my old comrade-in-arms Bill Clinton, whose speech in tribute to Helmut Kohl was the most remarked upon of the event, invited me to come back with him to New York. The main argument he had presented to the assembled dignitaries emphasized the need to keep Europe's doors open, and insisted that the Western world must be united in confronting the difficulties that face us all; this was music to the ears of the Europeans present. With his big boots, Trump had trampled all over the European carpet, proclaiming a return to isolationism. This message was not well received by countries that had emerged from two great wars to create for their nations a common space based on compromise and cooperation. This construction, Europe, has produced an uninterrupted seventy-two years of peace and prosperity, the longest period of peace in the history of the continent.

Beyond that, Bill was very lucid in his analysis of Hillary's defeat, recognizing that the intervention of the then director

Premier Maurice Duplessis, surrounded by the 1955 graduating class of the Séminaire de Trois-Rivières. My great friend Jean Pelletier is second from the right.

A memorable fishing expedition in northeastern Siberia in 1971. Proof that there are lots of fish in that part of the world!

Five prime ministers in a single photo: Pierre Elliott Trudeau, John Turner, Lester B. Pearson and myself, beneath a portrait of Sir Wilfrid Laurier.

The First Ministers' Conference on the Constitution, September 1980, with
Claude Charron and René Lévesque. On my left are Prime Minister Pierre Elliott
Trudeau and my colleague Allan MacEachen.

Anthony Vincent (1949–2008), former Canadian ambassador to Peru.
An unsung hero.

With my close advisers Eddie Goldenberg and Jean Pelletier, a few hours after my election as prime minister, October 25, 1993.

At the Élysée Palace, with President François Mitterrand.

Two experienced parliamentarians who respect each other . . . Joe Clark remains a friend.

With Fidel Castro in a Russian limousine in Havana, 1998. We spent 45 minutes stopped under a bridge.

With Tony Blair, then prime minister of Great Britain, and his wife, Cherie. She's the only woman I can call "chérie" without my wife, Aline, objecting.

President Jacques Chirac preferred beer to wine, to the amazement of our other guests.

A round of golf with President Clinton at Mont-Tremblant.

At the G7 meeting in Birmingham, England, in May 1998, Bill Clinton and I escaped from our bodyguards. Even though I'm twelve years older than the American president, I got over the wall more easily than he did. Those were the days when he ate more hamburgers…

With my wife, Aline, at the Mauricie National Park.

Bill Clinton and I got along like a couple of schoolboys.

▶ Lucien Bouchard and me. For once, we were on the same page. . .

One of my many meetings with Her Majesty Queen Elizabeth II. She truly likes to laugh.

Deep in conversation with my friend Helmut Schmidt, now sadly missed, former chancellor of the Federal Republic of Germany.

The former British prime minister John Major, a close ally.

A moving audience with Pope John Paul II.

At a performance of the rock opera *Starmania* in Paris with President François Mitterand, as well as lyricist Luc Plamondon.

of the FBI, James Comey, had been the turning point. It was not much consolation, but I was still happy to be able to tell him that if the Canadian provinces had been ten American states and able to vote, Hillary would have won the election easily, becoming the first woman to lead the greatest power in the Western world. About 70 percent of Canadians, in fact, supported this exceptional woman, who is also a good friend of Aline's and mine.

31

JULY 23, 1967: THE DAY IT ALL CHANGED

Today, July 15, 2017, we are just a few days from the fifti-eth anniversary of the provocative "Vive le Québec libre" that President Charles de Gaulle launched from the balcony of Montreal city hall. I believe that this was the opening shot that signalled a radical change in political debate in Quebec. As of July 23, 1967, the debate within the province was deeply marked by the division between those who wanted to make Quebec an independent country separate from Canada, and those who felt, on the contrary, that there was a better future for the francophone province within a vast country with extraordinary potential, Canada.

Marcel Chaput had sparked the debate on Quebec's sepa-ration ten years earlier, with limited success. Pierre Bourgault followed, with his party the Rassemblement pour l'indépend-ence national (RIN), which had more success. He was a remarkable orator, and young people drank in his words with great enthusiasm. He foresaw a clear and complete separation from Canada, with no compromise with the rest of the country. With great honesty he asserted, "It's not a question of economic well-being; it's a question of national pride. We will have our country, and then we will solve the problems caused by separation, one by one." He had the courage to propose a clear option, although there was also a certain bravado in the positions he took. It was all both exciting and dangerous.

I personally believe that he proposed the best formula, with a clear and uncompromising stance. But then René Lévesque appeared in the debate, with his soft separatism based on a step-by-step strategy devised by Claude Morin, to be rolled out according to the mood of the moment.

In 1966, Daniel Johnson, leader of the Union Nationale party, articulated a vision based on his call for "Égalité ou Indépendance," "Equality or Independence," and was able to defeat Premier Jean Lesage, who was thought to be unbeatable. René Lévesque, a minister in his cabinet, then completed the separatist change in direction by leaving the Liberal Party to form what became the Parti Québécois. The Union Nationale was devastated when Daniel Johnson died in 1968, precipitating a premature end to his party, despite the honourable efforts of his successors Jean-Jacques Bertrand and my friend Gabriel Loubier.

One day, when I was working as parliamentary secretary to the minister of finance, Mitchell Sharp, I received a visit from a young economist, a bureaucrat in our department, called Robert Bourassa. He wanted to talk to me about politics, he said, but soon he informed me that he was thinking of entering political life and had been sought out as a candidate for the 1966 election by Jean Lesage's Liberals. Before meeting him, I already knew that he was regarded as an intelligent and competent worker with a very promising future in the department. Because I loved my own life in politics, I naturally encouraged him to take the plunge. He told me that Premier Jean Lesage had offered him a choice of two ridings, Saint-Laurent or Mercier. I saw immediately that he had very high ambitions, so I advised him that his political career would be more promising if he ran in the totally francophone riding of Mercier, rather than the largely anglophone Saint-Laurent. He opted for Mercier, even though it was more difficult to win, and succeeded, becoming a member of the provincial legislature in 1966 and launching an exceptional career. Four years later, he succeeded Jean Lesage as head of the Quebec Liberal Party and, a few months after that, won the 1970 provincial election, becoming the youngest premier in the history of Quebec.

Over the following twenty-five years, our paths crossed many times, with some pleasant moments, and others that were not so agreeable. For example, during the 1980 referendum he offered to take a public role in the debate, partly out of a sense of duty and partly because he had been out of office and intended to return to the political stage. But Claude Ryan, the Liberal leader of the opposition in the National Assembly, did not want him around. Bourassa shared his disappointment with me.

I thought M. Ryan was making a mistake, because I knew that Bourassa was well respected in the province as an economist, and with that in mind I invited him to a No meeting at Grand-Mère in my electoral riding, without informing Ryan. His remarks at the meeting were effective, very professional and to the point, and he attracted a good deal of attention. During the following weeks he criss-crossed the province, and his success at those appearances opened the door to his return to politics in 1983, as the head of the Quebec Liberal Party, then as premier with the 1985 election.

When Brian Mulroney's proposal for constitutional reform, the Meech Lake Agreement, was being debated, I found myself in the No camp, along with Pierre Elliott Trudeau. At that point, despite the bonds we had forged over time, Bourassa forgot the past and our friendship died. The problem between us derived from the fact that he was a politician whose positions were always ambiguous. He was a federalist, but ... Separation? "No, but ..." For many of us, on all sides of the political equation, this became frustrating after a time. In any case, he remained elusive to the end.

On my arrival at Laval University as a student, I had joined the Laval Liberal Club and soon became president. I participated in the 1956 provincial election and made many speeches for my party's candidates in the Mauricie valley. I was very active in all the party's debates, and I rubbed shoulders with ministers, members, and even on a few occasions the Rt Hon. Louis St. Laurent, prime minister of Canada.

At the provincial election of 1956, Premier Maurice Duplessis wanted at all costs to defeat our member René Hamel, who never stopped attacking him in the National Assembly. Hamel was by far the most effective of all the opposition members, and probably better prepared than his colleagues because he was a lawyer who had graduated brilliantly from the University of Louvain in Belgium. After four years as a federal MP with the Bloc Populaire between 1945 and 1949, he was in a very good position to put Duplessis on the defensive. However, much to the annoyance of the Liberals, Duplessis managed to convince Gaston Hardy, the very popular mayor of Shawinigan, to leave the Liberal ranks and to join with him as a Union Nationale candidate. The Liberals who had supported Hardy for mayor saw his switch to the Union Nationale as a betrayal. This was an election such as you do not often see, with two high-quality candidates engaged in a passionate public argument. It was truly my first election: I gave no fewer than twenty speeches at the side of René Hamel. What a fantastic opportunity for a twenty-two-year-old!

The bridge over the Saint Maurice River in Shawinigan was in a very bad state. It was important because it joined Shawinigan proper to South Shawinigan, and the municipal authorities had been demanding a new bridge for years. The rumour was that *le Chef* would do nothing as long as René Hamel was the member in that part of the world. Duplessis came to the riding in person to confirm this: "If you want a bridge," he said, "you'll have to vote for my party, for Gaston

Hardy." With the verve and colourful language he was known for, he made his position very clear, stating, "No Gaston, no bridge." I replied in my speeches, with equal determination, "If we have to, we'll swim across, but never on our knees." That was how I began my fifty-year career in public speaking. René Hamel was re-elected, and when Jean Lesage formed his Liberal government in 1960, the first new bridge that was constructed was in Shawinigan.

It was at that time that I met René Lévesque, the famous host of the television show *Point de Mire* on Radio-Canada. When Lesage convinced him to be a Liberal candidate in the 1960 provincial election, we young Liberals thought that it was a master stroke. He ran successfully for the riding of Montréal-Laurier and I met him often after that, until my election as a federal member on April 8, 1963.

My provincial colleague René Hamel was minister of justice in the Lesage cabinet, and had agreed in the autumn of 1964 to become a Superior Court judge, leaving his seat in the National Assembly vacant. At the beginning of December René Lévesque called and told me that Lesage had put him in charge of the by-election to replace Hamel, and that he would like to meet with me in that connection. He took me to lunch at the Château Laurier on the Grande Allée in Quebec City. As the entire region of Mauricie had only one Liberal member, he said, they had to win this by-election in Saint-Maurice at all costs, and he proposed that I should give up my seat in Ottawa to join Jean Lesage's "équipe de tonnerre," his "super team." I was surprised, and reminded him that I had just been elected to Ottawa, and everything was going well for me at the House of Commons. I was heading a committee at the age of thirty, and I had a future where I was. He told me, "Jean, there's no future for you in Ottawa, because in five years the federal government will no longer exist for us. Join us now, and you'll have a very interesting future." This allusion to Quebec's separating from Canada, when he was a minister in Lesage's government, stunned me. I immediately shot back, "What—René, are you a separatist? Well, I'm not!"

Lévesque replied, "Okay, forget that, let's go and meet the premier." Clearly, Jean Lesage was expecting our visit, and he received me very warmly. I had known him when he was a minister in Louis St. Laurent's federal cabinet, and saw him again regularly at Liberal Party events. I remember very well what he said at the end of our conversation in Lévesque's presence. He recited a phrase from the Bible for the second week of Advent: "Now learn a parable of the fig tree; When his branch is yet tender, and putteth forth leaves, ye know that summer is nigh." It was December 1964. I asked him to give me some time to think. Take your time, he said.

Back in Ottawa, my prime minister, Lester B. Pearson, invited me into his office after Question Period. Being called on by the prime minister when you're a young thirty-year-old member is very surprising. He told me that Maurice Sauvé (the husband of Jeanne), who was then forestry minister, had informed him that René Lévesque was saying I was going to quit my seat to run for election at the provincial level, and that for him and our team, this was very bad news. In fact, at that time, the Liberal government was going through a bad phase; accusations of scandal were coming from all sides, and although none of them had ever been proven, they were eroding our popularity because two Quebec ministers were implicated. After a few minutes of discussion, the prime minister asked me, "Jean, do you believe in Canada? If so, I believe that a young man like you, with a future, should not leave." The fact that Pearson, my prime minister and a Nobel Prize winner, was appealing to me in these terms made a deep impression on me, and without a second's hesitation I replied that I was not going to Quebec. "Jean," he said, "this decision is too important. Take a week to reflect." So I went back to Shawinigan to consult with my friends and family. Everyone seemed to assume that I would choose to represent the region as a Quebec minister. Of twenty people I consulted, seventeen advised me to go to Quebec City, and only three thought it would be better to keep my seat in Ottawa: the lawyer Marcel Crête, the union leader Fernand D. Lavergne, and Aline. I took the minority's advice, and events would show that I had made the right decision, to the great satisfaction of Prime Minister Pearson.

When I told René Lévesque of my decision, he expressed his disappointment but asked me all the same to help win the by-election for which he was responsible. And then he asked me who, in my opinion, would be the best candidate to represent the party. I replied that I would look into it, and a few days later I told him that the best candidate was probably Dr. Clive Liddle, who was very well liked and a strong Liberal partisan. I told him that Dr. Liddle was of Irish ancestry and spoke French with an English accent, but that 95 percent of his patients were francophone. Lévesque's response was that an anglophone candidate in Saint-Maurice was not acceptable, and we had to find someone else. So I approached a friend, the notary Jean-Guy Trépanier, who agreed to present himself at the convention against Liddle. I directed my very effective team to work for Trépanier, who became the candidate and was duly elected the provincial member for Saint-Maurice.

Then what was bound to happen, happened: Liddle and his friends were furious with me, rightly, and at the following federal election Liddle ran against me for the NDP. Many of my organizers, all francophone, left me to help Liddle give me a good fight. I still won the election, but my dear friend Dr. Liddle had taught me a good lesson.

A few days later I went to the doctor's house, and he received me very politely. I told him I had come to apologize for the dirty trick I had played on him regarding the by-election, that I had been wrong to follow René Lévesque's advice, and he was to be congratulated on his courageous stand in getting back at me; he was a man with backbone and deserved all my respect.

When I think of that anglophone doctor, hard-working, competent, devoted, and popular, who had come to practise his profession among the francophones in my riding, and what I did to him, I am not proud of myself. I say to myself now what I said to him then: "Clive, you're a good man!"

32

THE LONGEST SUMMER OF MY LIFE

Referendum night, May 1980: after attending a celebra-
tory rally in Verdun, Aline and I returned late to the
hotel, absolutely exhausted. The next day I got up, with great
difficulty, to go to the office, and when I arrived I was immediately summoned by Prime Minister Trudeau. He thanked
me for having led the defence of the Liberal cause with success, and took the opportunity to tell me that I had to leave
that afternoon or the next day to make a start on a series of
consultations with all the provincial premiers. Oh là là! This
was no small task, when I'd just criss-crossed the province of
Quebec, day after day, going from city to city, from village to
village, over the forty days of the campaign.

Without any rest, I got on a plane to Toronto to meet Bill
Davis, the premier, and some other ministers; the next day
it was Winnipeg, Regina, Edmonton, and Victoria. The third
day it was back east to Halifax, followed by Charlottetown,
St. John's, and Fredericton. My mission was to impress on
the premiers the importance of fulfilling the prime minister's

promise to patriate the Constitution and draw up a Charter of Rights and Freedoms for every Canadian citizen. After the tour, I undertook a summer of consultations with the provincial departments of justice and/or intergovernmental affairs. From the very first meeting I saw that the task would be enormous.

Quebec's delegation was made up of the ministers Claude Morin, Louise Beaudoin, and Claude Charron. Charron was young and very engaging. His style came right out of Montreal's working class; he wasn't the sort to be subtle about his intentions, and that put me at ease. During a break in our discussions, I mentioned that the polls showed our fellow Québécois in favour of the patriation of the Constitution and the inclusion of a Charter of Rights by a margin of 80 percent. I thought we could come to a fair agreement. Bluntly, he replied, "Listen, Jean, our primary goal is the separation of Quebec. We'll play along with these consultations, but we can never sign a new constitution of Canada." He couldn't have been more clear. After talking with Trudeau, I continued the consultations, hoping that all the provinces would join with us and that we could persuade the Parti Québécois government to respect the popular will. I told Trudeau that it was a long shot but that we would be blamed if we didn't try. This was the longest summer of my life.

In the month of August, when I was at Parliament Hill with my father, we ran into the prime minister at the entrance to the House of Commons. Although Papa had met Trudeau before, for the former paper mill worker to meet the head of government was always something special. But then Trudeau said, "M. Chrétien, if I did not have your son at my side, I don't know what I'd do. He won the referendum for me, and now he's going to solve my constitutional problems." For Papa, who was then ninety-two years old, this compliment was beyond his expectations, and he could not accept it completely. I was very proud of his reply: "Prime Minister, if you and Jean cannot solve the constitutional problem, then no one can."

Back home that night it was as if he were twenty years younger. We talked politics for a long time with Aline, and before going to bed my father confessed, in a tone of voice both serious and reserved, "You know, Jean, I've never paid you compliments, but I have to say that I find you really not bad at all. . . ." In those days it was not customary to openly express one's feelings, and this was a unique gesture on his part. That night, when he finally went up to his room, he was in seventh heaven. This was our last meeting. A month later a heart attack brought him down. That meeting with my friend Pierre was probably the high point of his political memories. He left us a happy man . . . this man to whom I owe so much!

33

A LONG-LASTING LEGEND

L eading the federal troops during the 1980 referendum,
and immediately after that to be appointed minister
responsible for the patriation of the Constitution and the
development of the Charter of Rights: these were the most
difficult tasks that my boss Pierre Elliott Trudeau would ever
ask me to assume. The prime minister had called a meeting
of the provincial premiers to come to an agreement on the
terms for the patriation of the Constitution, which was still a
statute of the British Parliament in Westminster. The meeting took place November 4–5, 1981, at the Ottawa Conference
Centre. Much has been written on this subject and on the
role I played, with the assistance of Roy Romanow of
Saskatchewan and Roy McMurtry of Ontario, but I find that
historians and commentators have not given Bill Davis, the
Ontario premier at the time, the credit that he deserves.

Given the apparent impossibility of getting the premiers
to agree, Trudeau was ready to call an immediate halt to
the meeting. But I begged him to adjourn the session until

the next morning to give me a bit more time, which he finally agreed to do. I went back with Romanow to the Conference Centre kitchen to tell him that given the situation, Prime Minister Trudeau was prepared to suspend the talks and to go himself to London as the representative of the federal government in order to clear away the roadblocks to constitutional reform that had been in place since 1931. And if the British Parliament continued to be resistant to the idea, he was determined to take whatever measures were needed to unilaterally declare Canada's legal independence. I told Romanow what I thought we could obtain from Trudeau. The New Democrat said that as he was the only provincial minister who was not a Conservative, we would have to persuade the Ontarian Roy McMurtry to join forces with us. And so the three of us worked out the famous "kitchen compromise." When we left at around 6:30 p.m., I said to the two Roys, "Go and sell that to the provincial premiers. I have a harder task—I have to sell it to Trudeau."

At about nine o'clock I was at 24 Sussex to meet the prime minister, who had five or six ministers with him, and for an hour I was unable to convince him to approve the compromise measures: the notwithstanding clause and the amending formula. Most of the ministers present shared the prime minister's frustration and wanted to go to London without the provinces. Around ten o'clock, Trudeau left us to take a telephone call. When he came back he asked me a few more questions in a more conciliatory tone, and adjourned the meeting. As I was preparing to leave with the others, Trudeau took my arm to hold me back and led me into another room. To my great surprise, he said, "If you can get the support of seven provinces representing 50 percent of the population, I think I can accept your proposal. Let me sleep on it." We agreed to meet for breakfast the next morning. When I got back home at around eleven o'clock, Aline told me that Garde Gardom, the British Columbia minister of intergovernmental relations, had called me three times in the past hour. I returned his call, and he asked me if what Romanow and McMurtry were saying was true, and I assured him it was. He then told me that British Columbia would accept the compromise, and that Saskatchewan, Ontario, and the four Maritime provinces were also in agreement. "Well, Chrétien," he said, "you have your constitution. . . ."

Even though I was confident we now had a plan acceptable to Trudeau, I have to admit that I did not sleep well, to Aline's dismay. At breakfast, Prime Minister Trudeau confirmed his agreement. But the one who had really broken the deadlock was Bill Davis. It was he who had phoned Trudeau the night before. He told him that he accepted the compromise I had set in motion, but if Trudeau did not agree to it, he and Premier Hatfield, the only two provincial ministers to support it up to that time, would abandon ship. As premier of Ontario he represented almost 40 percent of the Canadian population, and he had strongly supported Trudeau's project from the very beginning, even in the face of opposition from all the other Conservative premiers except Hatfield of New Brunswick. Without Bill Davis's decisive intervention, I would never have been able to convince Pierre Elliott Trudeau. I've wanted to tell this story because Bill Davis has never had the recognition he deserves. "You must render unto Caesar the things that are Caesar's."

After breakfast, when Trudeau and I were being driven to the last session of the Federal-Provincial Conference, feeling that we had succeeded, he told me in very friendly fashion, "When I think that all these people believe you're not sufficiently educated. . . ." "When I think," I retorted, "that all these people think you're *too* educated. . . ." It was a memorable moment of closeness and complicity.

Over the last decades, I've told the story of this agreement many times, but some among the press prefer sulphurous conspiracy theories to the plain truth. That is what gave rise to the invention of "the night of the long knives": a fiction, nothing more. It's a legend that won't die, and a striking example of a myth that has been created and accepted as fact with absolutely no regard for reality.

34

MY MENTOR, MITCHELL SHARP

When I think about it, I am astonished: if I had not had Réal Caouette's Créditistes as adversaries when I was first elected, I probably wouldn't have had the same career.

After my election on April 8, 1963, I set out for Ottawa, travelling first to Montreal by car with Jean-Paul Gignac, then boarding the train to my destination. Gignac was a very well-informed businessman, close to René Lévesque, who had named him commissioner of Hydro Quebec. As of 1966, he held the post concurrently with that of CEO of Sidbec, the Quebec government steel corporation. His grandfather had been mayor of Shawinigan, owner of a very prosperous family business, and politically a Liberal. Our two families knew each other well, and the Gignacs were among the most generous contributors to my electoral war chest. During our drive that Monday morning, I told him that I found Caouette's remarks about the Bank of Canada very intriguing. Jean-Paul gave me the following advice: "As you're very young, why not learn about finance? It's a subject in which

French Canadians generally show very little interest." Once at the office, I had to reply to a questionnaire from the prime minister concerning new members' preferences for the different parliamentary committees on which we might serve. I made my first choice finance, and immediately became a member of the Banks and Finance Committee.

At the time of the 1965 election, I was parliamentary secretary to Prime Minister Pearson. Immediately after the election, the prime minister told me that he wanted me to work with the finance minister, Mitchell Sharp, because I was the only MP who had chosen finance, and that if I continued to work hard, I might one day become the first French-Canadian finance minister of Canada. Pearson's prediction came true in 1977, when I indeed became minister of finance.

And so if Réal Caouette had not prompted me to talk about the money supply, the control of the banks, and the Bank of Canada during the 1963 election campaign, my life might have taken a different turn.

Mitchell Sharp was then a Toronto MP and minister of finance. He became my mentor. At the age of twenty-eight, when he was an economist working for the grain industry in Winnipeg, he left his job to become a volunteer with a symbolic salary of one dollar a year in order to contribute to the war effort. That was how he got in the door of the federal government system.

After the war Mitchell Sharp joined the Department of Commerce and climbed up the ladder to become deputy minister to the all-powerful C.D. Howe. In 1958, after a conflict with Prime Minister Diefenbaker, he left the public service to become a successful businessman. When Lester B. Pearson became leader of the Liberal Party, he asked Sharp to organize the famous Kingston conference to set the party on the progressive path that was to be the Liberals' trademark for decades to come. At the 1962 election he was chosen to run against the finance minister Donald Fleming, and lost the election by a very small margin. Nine months later he was finally elected in Fleming's place. For me, to be instructed by a man of Mitchell Sharp's calibre was a better education than years spent in even the best university. I was present at all the meetings with the senior officials of the Finance Department and the Bank of Canada. Every Monday, Tuesday, and Thursday, we had to be on Parliament Hill to vote, because we were a minority government and every vote counted. I was like part of the furniture in his office, and we spent hours every evening discussing the day's problems, the ins and outs of public administration and politics. If Bill Clinton could write, "I know no one who knows as much about the art of governing as Jean Chrétien," it is because I had as my private teacher and mentor my great friend Mitchell Sharp, whom I can never thank enough for his immense contribution to our nation's public life.

In 1968, after the excellent Mike Pearson stepped down as leader of the Liberal Party, Mitchell Sharp presented himself as a candidate to replace him, and as was proper, I decided to support him. When Justice Minister Pierre Elliott Trudeau threw his hat in the ring, his friend Jean Marchand, the minister responsible for Quebec, told me that all the Quebec ministers had to support Trudeau. I replied that I had promised to support Sharp, and so I was not going to obey him. He retorted that I risked losing my place in the cabinet if Trudeau was elected. I shot back that then I would be losing my place because I was a man of my word. "And if you were to name in my stead someone who does not keep his word, I'm not sure you would be very far ahead." Finally, Trudeau himself came to see me in my office, to seek my support. I told him that I thought that he would be a very good prime minister. That being said, I noted that when he and Robert Winters entered the race, Mitchell's support had begun to erode. And so I told him that if my candidate did not make the cut, he would be my second choice.

On the Monday of the Liberal Party's leadership convention, Mitchell, thorough as he was, had arranged an assessment by an impartial agency of the strength of his support, and the result was not promising. And so he went to his old friend Lester Pearson to announce his intention to quit the race. When he came back, he asked me to contact Pierre Trudeau. I succeeded in reaching his mother in Montreal, and I immediately organized a meeting between the two of them in Ottawa.

As I was co-chairman of Sharp's campaign along with the Ontario Liberal Party leader Robert Nixon, I had the responsibility of transferring our organization over to Trudeau. Ministers, members, and delegates supporting Sharp had almost all rallied to Trudeau. This gave his campaign a big boost, what with the arrival of important names such as Sharp, Jean-Luc Pépin, Bud Drury, George McIlwraith, and Bob Nixon. Three days before the vote, it was the perfect shot in the arm. During the entire leadership convention, at every public meeting, Sharp was asked to sit at Trudeau's right.

Many in the Liberal Party had wondered if it was really possible for them to choose this radical, this rebel, Trudeau as party leader and prime minister, but the reassuring presence of Mitchell Sharp by his side told them that yes, it was possible.

Everyone believed that Sharp had received Pearson's approval, and the fact that the ministers who were supporting him included the party's heavyweights gave the same impression. Trudeau won the race on the fourth ballot against Bob Winters—but if Sharp hadn't arrived at the right moment, would he have won?

Trudeau never reproached me for having kept my word. On the contrary, in April 1968 I began a marvellous journey of nearly fifteen years in the cabinet of Pierre Elliott Trudeau.

During my long career as minister, leader of the opposition, and prime minister, when I had difficult problems I paid a visit to Mitchell Sharp at his home to seek his advice. He could usually raise my morale. His second wife, the devoted Jeannette Dugal, always welcomed me with great kindness. After an hour or more of discussion, he sometimes went to the piano and played me Chopin, Liszt, Mozart, and other classics. I turned the pages of his score, and at the end, I went home to take up the burden that was sometimes difficult to bear.

When I became his parliamentary secretary in 1965, as of the very first day, he invited me to take part in a meeting where were present the deputy minister of finance, the governor of the Bank of Canada, and a few other highly placed civil servants. It was a question of taxes, of deficits, of borrowing on the market, of interest rates, and everything of course took place in English. At the end of the meeting, Mitchell said to me, "Jean, don't forget that everything you've heard here is very confidential, and you must talk about it to no one." I replied, "Don't worry, Mitchell, I didn't understand a thing!" That was quite a beginning!

When he became a candidate for leader of the party, my colleague in the neighbouring riding, the member for Champlain, Jean-Paul Matte, invited him into our region, where he addressed the mayor with a text prepared in French. He did very well. The same thing for the priest and some citizens in the rectory, but when we arrived at a rather noisy Knights of Columbus sugar shack celebration, things got more complicated. We had not planned a speech by the minister of finance, but when the celebrants began to cry "We want Sharp, we want Sharp!" Mitchell did not want to improvise without a text. And so to relax him, I asked Jean-Paul Matte to serve him his trademark cocktail made from illegal home-brew and maple syrup. It was called a "réduit." Mitchell drank a good quantity, to the applause of the crowd.

A little later, my Mitchell was up on a table improvising his first speech in the language of Molière.

When he retired in 1978, his friends and supporters organized a fine evening during which they expressed their gratitude, and made him the gift of an electric organ for his cottage. The next day at the cabinet meeting, the prime minister asked the minister of defence, Barney Danson, to give an account of the evening that paid homage to Mitchell. Danson, who could be very funny, ended his remarks by asserting that everything had been a big success, and that Mitchell was "a very happy man," in retirement with a new wife and a "new organ." Everyone burst out laughing. . . .

35

A MEMORABLE VACATION IN MEXICO

I t was another formal evening at Rideau Hall, the official residence of the governor general, who at the time was Adrienne Clarkson, a refugee from Hong Kong and former journalist for the CBC's English network, very learned and sophisticated, whom I had named to this post—one of my best nominations as prime minister.

The guest of honour was a foreign head of state, and when I was asked to say a few words, wanting to inject a little humour I said that Canada was being led, de facto, by three women: the governor general, Adrienne Clarkson; the chief justice of the Supreme Court, Beverley McLachlin, who was present; and my wife, Aline. Of course, everyone smiled. Later on, Justice McLachlin, the first female chief justice of the Supreme Court, made use of this witticism in her public speeches.

In fact, I was most serious when I talked about Aline, because I always tell anyone who is listening that I would never have had the career I did without the woman I've always called my "Rock of Gibraltar" at my side.

What is not so well known, though, is that Aline came into my life because of another woman, who also had a significant impact on my life. That was my mother, Marie, who spared no effort in ensuring that Aline would become the woman of my life.

I was eighteen years old, with a summer job at the Belgo paper mill, when my brother Michel phoned me from the Valcartier military base where he was spending the summer as a Canadian Army cadet. He told me that he'd invited ten of his friends to spend Saturday night in Shawinigan, and ordered me to find girls to go with them to the dance hall, "La Plage Idéale," at Lac-à-la-Tortue. I replied that was impossible, timorous as I was when it came to the opposite sex. Never mind, over the following days I applied myself with my usual tenacity, and to my amazement I was able to complete the assignment I was given by the importunate Michel.

I asked all the girls I knew—and some I didn't—and then I spotted on the bus this very pretty girl, Aline, and I asked her if she would accompany a young cadet to the Saturday night dance at the Plage Idéale. She said that she might go, but not with a stranger, only with me, if her mother gave her permission. She was then barely sixteen. The next day, very sheepish, she came to tell me that her mother had refused her permission. Seeing her discomfort, I told her that it didn't matter, and that I'd like to go to the movies with her the next evening. She accepted immediately and I was absolutely thrilled. It was the first time I'd gone to the movies with a girl, and that was sixty-six years ago, the second week of August 1952. It was the beginning of a beautiful love story that endures today.

When I met her I was a hyperactive and very undisciplined young man who caused problems for everyone, which worried my mother a great deal. With this new girlfriend I suddenly became more serene, to the great delight of my mother, who decided then and there that I was at all costs to fall in love with the sweet Aline. When September arrived and I was compelled to return to school in Trois-Rivières, Maman sometimes came to visit me at the college. She also began to invite Aline to keep her company on her bus trip. They came to the college to liberate me for a few hours on Sunday afternoon, the only day of the week when that was permitted. Once outside the college I met Aline, and Maman left us to spend some time with her cousins who lived in Trois-Rivières. Aline and I spent these few hours, as in Georges Brassens's song, "smooching on the park benches, . . . paying no mind to the looks from decent passersby."

At five o'clock Aline left me to board the bus with Maman and return to Shawinigan. All my schoolmates thought Maman was very modern, and they envied me.

My mother's strategy worked wonders, and I fell deeply in love with Aline, which radically changed my behaviour. I became much more disciplined, and I started to have good grades again. I had to, or I wouldn't have been allowed my monthly day off, when I could spend the day in Shawinigan and see Aline. I became almost, as they say, as good as gold.

On September 10, 1957, during my second year of law at Laval University, we got married, and we spent two marvellous years, me as a student, she as a secretary, poor and happy in the wonderful city of Quebec. Maman had good instincts, and the son she feared might become the black sheep of the family in fact became the serious and ambitious lawyer of whom she had dreamed—all thanks to Aline.

During the rest of my life, at every turn of the road, Aline was there to help me, to advise me, to keep me in line, to give me a push at just the right moment.

Here are a few anecdotes that demonstrate this well. For example, the decision I view as the most important of my life, other than my marriage proposal, was my choice to remain a federal MP, resisting the advances of Jean Lesage and René Lévesque, who were urging me to switch to the provincial arena. As I mentioned before, Aline was one of just three people who gave me the right advice: to stay with Lester B. Pearson.

In April 1968, when I was finance minister, Aline and I took a week-long vacation in Zihuatanejo in Mexico, and when we got to our room, we realized that Jacques Parizeau and his wife, Alice, were our neighbours. I must say that we all had a very good time. We ate together, we went fishing, we walked on the beach. Jacques's wife, Alice Parizeau, born in Poland, was an exceptional person. Jacques was very courteous, and to my astonishment, at dinner in the evening he wore his very British jacket à la Rudyard Kipling, even though we were on the beach.

Trudeau was now the leader of the Liberal Party. I was still the minister of the Department of National Revenue, and since Jacques was an economic consultant for both federal and provincial governments, there was much to discuss. A few times, M. Parizeau (as I always called him) told me that it would be hard for me to understand something he was saying because I had not had the privilege, like him, of studying at the London School of Economics. He was not over-burdened by humility. I smiled and, in general, things went smoothly. But the day before our departure, we were having lunch together, and just when I thought my arguments were particularly convincing, he intervened to serve up, not very politely, his usual remark about the London School. His wife, thinking he was going a bit far, said, "When I met Jacques he was a very handsome young man but also extremely rude." Jacques, seeing what he had done and wanting to apologize, added, "I'm not such a handsome fellow now, but I'm still rude." Aline, a rather shy woman and normally very reserved, burst out, "That's exactly what I was going to say, monsieur!" Oh là là. What a shock! Jacques excused himself, claiming he had to work. When we were back in our room, Aline was very embarrassed, but I reassured her and told her, "I've never loved you more than at that moment!"

Despite this incident, we remained good friends. Some years later, when Alice Parizeau had become a *grande dame* if ever there was one, she visited Aline in Ottawa and told her how much she and Jacques cherished the memory of our stay on the Mexican Pacific coast—as did Aline and I.

In 1976 Parizeau became the Quebec finance minister, and the next year I too became finance minister, in Pierre Trudeau's government, even though unlike Parizeau and Trudeau I'd never attended the London School of Economics. Everything went well between us, despite our significant political differences. But matters took a more difficult turn when I decided to table a budget in collaboration with my provincial colleagues, which was unheard of. Over dinner in a Montreal hotel with Darcy McKeough, the Ontario treasurer, Jacques Parizeau, and me, we agreed that to stimulate the economy, it would be good to reduce the provincial sales tax by 3 percent, and as there was no federal sales tax, the federal government would pay two-thirds of that. I then obtained the consent of the other eight provinces. Imagine my surprise then to receive a phone call from Parizeau saying that the agreement was off because it had been rejected by René Lévesque and his cabinet. He said, "We're going to take the money and spend it as we see fit." I replied that I had made commitments to the other provinces, and if Quebec didn't follow suit, the federal government would not send the money. I told him that if he couldn't keep his word, I would respect mine, as given to the other nine provinces. Then the fireworks began. I decided to send eighty-five dollars to every Quebec taxpayer, and nothing to the Quebec government. The following days were probably the most difficult of my political career. At one point, on a Wednesday morning when Aline came to wake me, I told her that I wasn't getting up, that I'd gambled and lost, and that my career was over. I was truly discouraged. A few minutes later, she came back into the bedroom, and for the first and last time in our life as a couple, she brought me my breakfast in bed, and told me to continue to fight.

She had brought me out of my funk, and I returned to Parliament. The budget devised in concert with the provinces was a success in the nine other provinces, with Quebec going it alone. The eighty-five-dollar cheque for each taxpayer was welcomed by most Quebec families, and a Gallup poll showed a 3 percent increase in Liberal support. If I had resigned that day of my breakfast in bed, my time as finance minister and my political career would have ended abruptly after fifteen years of public life. I would never have become prime minister. And so, when I told foreign leaders that Canada was led by three women, for me, and perhaps for the country, the most important was the third, the only one who ever served me breakfast in bed, my Rock of Gibraltar, Aline.

36

PIERRE ELLIOTT TRUDEAU AND ME

T onight I take up my pen to write about the nineteen years
I spent in the federal parliament with one Pierre Elliott
Trudeau. I believe this chapter will be longer than the rest.

It was the election of autumn 1965, and Prime Minister
Pearson had invited me to go with him to his riding of
Algoma East, where he was launching his campaign. As I
was his parliamentary secretary and a francophone, I was to
speak primarily in French to the many francophones living in
his electoral district. The Conservatives were running against
him a star of TV and radio, Joel Aldred. All I knew about
him was that he was well known in the province and that he
drove a Rolls-Royce. To the delight of Mr. Pearson, I called
him Rolls-Royce Aldred.

We spent the second night of the tour in Espanola rather
than return to Ottawa, because the PM was a big sports fan
and he preferred watching a football game to being in an airplane. As we watched the game, he told me that he'd been able
to persuade Jean Marchand, the prominent Quebec union

leader; Gérard Pelletier, chief editorial writer for *La Presse*; and the intellectual Pierre Trudeau to join our team. He quietly added that the operation might delay my entry into the cabinet. I replied that if he had MPs more competent than myself, then he ought to name them first. Marchand and Pelletier were, in my opinion, important acquisitions, but to me Trudeau seemed more problematic. "Liberals," I said, "don't like him at all because of his repeated attacks on the Bomarc missiles in 1963, and given his blunt style, you're going to have trouble finding him a riding." Which was exactly what happened. Dr. Noël, the Outremont MP, absolutely refused to give up his seat; my friend Jean-Paul Matte was prepared to give over his riding of Champlain, but the riding executive rejected the idea out of hand. And so Mr. Pearson, who had appointed Alan McNaughton Speaker of the House in the Senate, offered him the riding of Mount Royal, where Pierre Trudeau had to work very hard to win the nomination over a young Liberal, Dr. Stuart Smith, who later became the leader of the Liberal Party in Ontario.

On November 8, 1965, the "Three Wise Men," Jean Marchand, Gérard Pelletier, and Pierre Elliott Trudeau, were elected to the House of Commons, and the press began to circulate the rumour that Marchand would replace Guy Favreau as the minister responsible for Quebec. Indeed, Marchand made his presence felt very rapidly, and a few weeks after the election, he asked me to find a "new guard" candidate to replace the chair of the Quebec caucus, viewed as belonging to the "old guard." On the day of the vote for chairman of the caucus, there was a tie that the departing chair broke by voting for the old guard candidate. When Marchand and I realized that Pierre Trudeau had not voted, we were furious. So I went to see Trudeau to tell him that his abstention had allowed the old guard to win, and that Marchand and I looked a bit foolish in light of this defeat. He replied, "Even if Marchand wanted Laniel, I don't know either of the candidates, and so I didn't vote." I replied that he'd better learn the ropes quickly, or he wouldn't go very far. You have to admit that he learned pretty fast.

A few months later, when he was parliamentary secretary to the prime minister, and I was the same for the finance minister, we accompanied Mitchell Sharp to a federal-provincial conference of finance ministers. At the end of the conference, Sharp sat down at a table to answer journalists' questions. Then, to my great surprise, Trudeau said to me, "Come on, Jean, we're going to stand just behind Sharp, and the journalists will see that we've participated in the conference." I told him jokingly that he was indeed learning fast, very fast.

After spending more than six years with Indian Affairs and Northern Development, and having served an apprenticeship that was invaluable to me all through my career, I was appointed by Trudeau, usually when there were unexpected difficulties, as chairman of the Treasury Board; minister of Industry and Commerce; minister of National Revenue; minister of Justice; and minister of Energy, Mines, and Resources. Each time, I was hard to persuade; I didn't want to change portfolios—except when he asked me to replace Donald Macdonald, who had suddenly left the Finance Department. Mr. Pearson had once said that if I worked hard and did well, I could become the first franco-phone finance minister. And so I accepted Trudeau's offer with relish, despite the fact that there was a downside. Trudeau in effect said that there was one condition: if I were needed to replace Robert Bourassa (who had been defeated by René Lévesque the year before), I could not refuse just because I was finance minister of Canada. In the end it was Claude Ryan who became the provincial Liberal leader, and I remained at my post in Ottawa, to my great relief.

Later, after his electoral victory in the spring of 1979, Prime Minister Joe Clark decided to put off till autumn his first Speech from the Throne, and his first budget was not presented until mid-November, when Pierre Trudeau had already announced his retirement as leader of the Liberal Party. The stupefying result of the vote on the Crosbie budget resulted in the fall of the still very new Conservative government, introducing a political dynamic that was utterly unprecedented. Trudeau had a difficult decision to make, because a surprise election was now on the horizon, and his party, taken unawares, found itself, de facto, with-out a leader.

In the hours preceding the historic vote, my friend Allan MacEachen met with Trudeau a number of times, and asked me to make sure that all the MPs would be present for that fateful decision. I told Trudeau and Allan that Social Credit was not going to vote with the Conservatives, ensuring the certain defeat of the Conservative government. MacEachen told Trudeau that if he did not receive any instructions to the contrary before 5 p.m., we were going to bring down the government. Between four and five o'clock I was alone with Allan in his office; both of us were on edge, awaiting our friend Pierre's decision. The telephone did not ring, and Canada's history changed course in dramatic fashion. The Conservative leader Joe Clark lost the election brought on by his failure in dealing with the Crosbie budget, and Trudeau became prime minister once again. Meanwhile René Lévesque, who had already confirmed the date for his referendum, based on the murky concept of "sovereignty-association," found himself, on May 20, 1980, facing Trudeau rather than Joe Clark. Sometimes silence is more eloquent than words.

Trudeau loved silence. During half the years when he was prime minister, I sat next to him in the House of Commons. He didn't like to "chat." Small talk was not his strong point, and when I became prime minister, he gave me some excellent counsel. He told me to reserve the prime minister's secondary residence in the Gatineau hills for rest, silence, and reflection. What good advice! During the decade when I was prime minister, the residence at Lac Mousseau, better known as Harrington Lake, was my peaceful haven. To succeed in the onerous task of governing a country, it is essential to set time aside for reflection. Several hours walking in the woods or paddling alone in a canoe are often hours better spent than at a lot of "briefings," or in frenetic posting on Twitter, as we can see today.

To speak properly of Pierre Elliott Trudeau, who was my colleague in the House of Commons for nineteen years, and my political boss and prime minister for sixteen years, would require a book all to itself. I had the opportunity to get to know him quite well during the eight years I sat beside him in the House of Commons and the cabinet. Much has been written about his personality, but what I know of him has remained fixed in my mind. He was serious, erudite, intolerant of frivolousness, but patient and generous with his ministers, and with me. I never quite understood why he trusted me so much. He was capable of delegating responsibilities but could not easily tolerate incompetence or laziness. Perhaps this anecdote best encapsulates his way of dealing with his subordinates: One day, when I was minister of Indian Affairs and Northern Development, I received a surprising phone call from him. "Jean, are you mad at me? Because I realize that you haven't talked to me for a whole year." "Not at all, why are you asking? I don't call you because I don't want to disturb you, and I'm happy that you don't feel obliged to call me. . . ." "I'm calling you to thank you for being the way you are. If my ministers were all like you, it would be easy to be prime minister."

For sixteen years Pierre Elliott Trudeau was my only boss. He entrusted me with enormous tasks, and sometimes the difficulties seemed insurmountable. He never raised his voice. When I was involved in serious political controversies,

we discussed them calmly and rationally. Without his understanding, his wisdom, his knowledge, and above all his
constant support, I would never have known the wonderful
career that was mine. What more can I say?

37

AN UNFORGETTABLE DAY
WITH THE CLINTONS

I t was an unforgettable day.

Invited by the family of the German Chancellor Helmut Kohl, and at the request of the federal government, I attended the funeral of the former chancellor on July 1, 2017. Bill Clinton was there as well, and as he was travelling on a private plane the day after the ceremony, I hitched a ride from Germany to New York with the former U.S. president. We spent eight hours together then, and I have to say that I was not bored for a moment in the company of this extremely erudite man who was quite fascinating to listen to. He told me that he was going to be vacationing with his wife, Hillary, their daughter, Chelsea, his son-in-law, and his two grandchildren in North Hatley, Quebec, and that he'd be happy to play a round of golf with me. Thus on Saturday, August 19, 2017, I spent a day with him that was both ordinary and absolutely exceptional. I very much like playing golf with friends, because to spend a few hours on a golf course, with no tele-phone, surrounded by nature, and with friendly people, is always a pleasure. It's rather rare to play golf with people you don't like, because you don't want to waste a day in nature, in idyllic surroundings, with unpleasant company.

On the other hand, with a partner like Bill Clinton, the day becomes truly memorable. I was up at six o'clock, and at seven I was driving along Highway 55 towards Sherbrooke. I arrived at the golf club at 9:30, the time we'd arranged. I was told that Clinton would be late, and I thought to myself that we would probably start the game at around eleven o'clock, because I knew his habits, and that's exactly when he arrived. During the lunch break, we were treated to a very interesting history lesson from an illustrious American citizen who'd been born in the South, had been governor of the state of Arkansas, and had some ancestors who were openly racist. We also learned about former presidents of the United States from the South who owned slaves, such as Washington and Jefferson. It was a fascinating lunch. And on such a glorious day!

The Clintons had been invited by Louise Penny, a writer from Quebec who is very popular in the United States. Her novels are set in the Eastern Townships, and many of her characters are French-Canadian, notably her Detective Gamache. The Clintons are fans of her books and so were happy to spend a week in these surroundings. Louise Penny invited them to visit the Benedictine monastery of Saint-Benoît-du-lac on Lake Memphremagog. Hillary and Bill were fascinated by their visit, by the atmosphere created by prayer, meditation, silence, and the peace of this magnificent place. It must be said, however, that the Prior of St-Benoît-du-lac made sure to tell them that the murder in the monastery that occurs in one of Louise Penny's books never actually took place.

At the end of the day, along with the Clinton family and fifteen or so of their friends, mostly from the United States, we attended a reception at the celebrated and very pleasant Hovey Manor in North Hatley. Governor Terry McAuliffe of Virginia joined us, though he was still preoccupied by the Charlottesville crisis that had exposed to us the true face of Donald Trump. Hearing Bill Clinton, the governor of Virginia, and other Americans present express their concern, their confusion, and their incomprehension, I saw how lucky I was to live in Canada, and how important it is for us to remain vigilant, because you never know. Sadly, no society is immune from backsliding where social values are concerned.

Happily, the atmosphere became festive again. As it was Bill Clinton's seventy-first birthday, the daughter of the celebrant, his charming Chelsea, stepped up with her adorable little girl, Charlotte. Not yet three years old, the child was holding a pretty cake with a lit candle and sang, "Happy birthday, Grandpa." Bill had tears in his eyes. It was very moving.

For this man, who had had a very difficult childhood with a tyrannical stepfather, it was certainly a sublime moment to find himself surrounded by an exceptional wife, a gifted daughter who resembles Hillary, a first-class son-in-law, and two adorable grandchildren.

During the dinner that followed, at which the hotel's chef presented a seven-course gourmet meal of the highest quality, I chatted with Hillary on my right and Louise Penny on my left, allowing me rich exchanges with two remarkable women. Hillary was the same woman with whom I had conversed when she was the American first lady and I was prime minister. She likes to laugh but is also very interested in questioning you on the vital issues of our time. Over seventeen years she had been secretary of state in the Obama administration and then a Democratic candidate for president in the 2016 election, and had received three million more votes than Donald Trump. Although she seemed disappointed by her defeat, she was not bitter. She was now very concerned about the political situation in her country. She said she was happy that Canada had a progressive prime minister like Justin Trudeau, who was very popular around the world, and she again questioned me about our national health system, as she had when I was still an active politician. Given the breadth of her learning, her intelligence, her experience, her absolute commitment to public service, I couldn't help thinking of what a president she would have been. It's very sad to observe the monumental error our neighbours to the south made in November of 2016!

I fear that Hillary's defeat, and the arrival of the fanatical Trump, mark the true end of the American Empire. You can understand why Aline and I are so happy to have the Clintons as friends, and almost as proud to be removed as far as possible from the unspeakable Donald Trump.

Ah yes! Surely you want to know who won the golf game at Lake Memphremagog? I have to tell you that that is a state secret. I can say, however, that I defended the Canadian nation honourably, despite my young eighty-three years, and especially when I executed a putt of over fifty feet! The Quebec caddies and members of the RCMP who were with us seemed very happy with their former prime minister, almost thirteen years older than President Clinton.

38

AIMING AT THE WRONG TARGET...

I mmediately after I left politics, at the very end of 2003, the internationally noted weekly magazine *The Economist* published an in-depth article on Canada to mark my departure, the cover featuring a moose wearing pink glasses, and the title "Canada Is Cool." In that issue, for the most part flattering to the team I'd led since 1993, *The Economist* provided an analysis of our ten years of government. A few years later, when David Cameron came to power in Britain, the *Financial Times* in London organized a meeting of businessmen with whom the British prime minister had collaborated along with his finance minister, George Osborne, referred to as the Chancellor of the Exchequer in the parliamentary tradition of his country. I was one of the guests of this prestigious group, where everyone wanted to know what we had done to go from a 6.2 percent deficit of gross national product to a budgetary surplus in only three years. The question I was asked most often was, "How were you able to impose that policy without provoking a strike in the public service?"

I told them that I was as surprised as they were to have achieved that tour de force without a single strike, and I had asked that same question directly of union leaders in the course of a meeting. Now, I don't know if it was a compliment or a criticism, but they replied that they knew nothing would change my mind and so had considered it futile to organize any strikes.

In the same spirit, at the end of the French president Jacques Chirac's mandate, his party asked to meet our ministers, MPs, and top officials to discuss Canada's success in eliminating budget deficits. This was not surprising, since delegations from several countries came to Ottawa with the same thing in mind, and the Clerk of the Privy Council, Jocelyne Bourgon, made dozens of presentations on the subject around the world after leaving public service. During my talk in Paris, someone asked me an off-topic question that led me to say something about French politics. The question was, "What do you think of Nicolas Sarkozy's election campaign?" I replied that I thought he was making a grave error in condemning his predecessor Jacques Chirac, from the same political family as himself, simply in order to set himself apart, rather than attacking his true adversary, Ségolène Royal. Most of the participants agreed, and I told them that it was up to them to pass on the message to Sarkozy, but it was suggested that it would be more effective if I were the one who talked to him. Before agreeing to go and see Sarkozy, I consulted my friend Jean Pelletier, who advised me to talk first to President Chirac.

That same evening I dined with Aline at the Élysée, and during the meal I asked Jacques Chirac if I ought to go and see Sarkozy as his party was urging me to do. Now, I saw very clearly that the president was not a fan of his future successor. Reeling off a series of negative epithets to describe Sarkozy, he ended by saying that I was wasting my time. However, his wife, Bernadette, totally disagreed. She said, "Jean, it's your duty to do it." Like any good husband, Jacques gave in to his wife's wishes, and the next day I went to see candidate Sarkozy. Right off, I told him that I thought he was making a mistake in attacking Chirac, and I added that Gore had run a campaign saying that he wasn't Bill Clinton, to which the Americans replied that indeed he wasn't, and he lost the election. Paul Martin also kept saying that he was not Jean Chrétien, and the same thing ended up happening to him. On the other side of the Channel, Gordon Brown insisted on saying that he was not Tony Blair, with the same result as the others. What's more, while the future president had a tendency to look down on Ségolène Royal, I told him that he ought not to underestimate her because she was the first female candidate for the presidency; she expressed herself very well, and besides, she was pretty. If he let her establish a lead, he might have a lot of trouble catching up. The next morning, when Aline and I returned to the airport, the National Assembly deputy Jérôme Chartier, who had accompanied me on my visit to Sarkozy the day before, showed me a newspaper and said, "He's listened to you—yesterday afternoon he attacked the Socialist candidate, and not Chirac."

I had also suggested that Sarkozy say that Chirac had written a great page in the history of France, and that he himself would write another—necessarily different, because he was a very different person—and he hoped that this page would be even greater.

I had seen John Turner make the same mistake as Gore, Martin, and Brown. He'd done everything possible to set himself apart from Pierre Elliott Trudeau in the 1984 election, but failed miserably in his campaign against Brian Mulroney. That was why, when I became leader of the Liberal Party in 1990, I had no hesitation in saying that I had served in the cabinet of P.E. Trudeau for fifteen years, and I accepted my responsibility for the decisions that were made, because no one can work with a prime minister for such a long time and then try to distance himself from him afterwards.

Perhaps those close to my own successor ought to have followed the same advice, as provided by the highly respected journalist Chantal Hébert in her column on June 18, 2003, in the *Toronto Star* shortly after my departure, when my level of approval was very high in Quebec in the wake of my decision on Iraq. In evaluating the potential for important Liberal gains in Quebec during the next election, she suggested that my successor ought to think long and hard before shunning me and my end-of-mandate legacy.

It's also interesting to note that the Australian prime minister John Howard, who had been in office for eleven years up to 2007, was not pleased with the behaviour of his finance minister, Peter Costello. Costello did nothing to hide his ambition to succeed him. Exasperated by this constant pressure, Howard decided to run a fifth time rather than to leave the road clear for his presumed successor. Result: his party, the Liberals, lost the election to the Labour Party, and he was defeated in his own riding. As for Costello, after the party's defeat he was offered the leadership, but declined, and left political life a little under two years later. He never became leader of the Liberal Party, never mind prime minister of Australia. And so it was all for nothing.

With Bill Gates, founder of Microsoft, and John Manley, minister of industry.

Nelson Mandela, whom I made an honorary citizen of Canada in 2001.

In my office with Nelson Mandela, who is
wearing an arrow sash for the occasion.

Mitchell Sharp (1911–2004) was a true mentor to me.

Vladimir Putin, who, it must be said, restored the pride of the Russian people.

I took care that my prime-ministerial desk was never buried under documents.

With the Aga Khan, in my office—
and not on his private island.

"A battle between two bears!" said Bill Clinton, seeing Boris Yeltsin and me in a tug of war.

With the German
chancellor Helmut Kohl
and MP Jack Anawak,
Nunavut, 1995.

NAFTA, before the Trump era . . . hand in hand with the Mexican president Vicente Fox, and his American counterpart, George W. Bush.

My wife, Aline, my rock of Gibraltar, and our faithful friend Bill Clinton, in Montreal in 2017.

A family portrait at the Summit of the Americas in Quebec City, 2001.

Maman, the famous sculpture by Louise Bourgeois, in front of the National Gallery of Canada in Ottawa.

Louise Bourgeois, *Maman*, 1999, cast 2003. Bronze, stainless steel and marble, 927 x 891 x 1024 cm
Collection of the National Gallery of Canada
© The Easton Foundation / SOCAN, Montreal (2018), Jonathan Hayward

The Kluane National Park in the Yukon.
A legacy of which I am proud.

Jaume Plensa, *Source*, 2017
Stainless steel, paint; 100 x 74 x 70 cm
© Jaume Plensa / SOCAN (2018), Ivanoh Demers

Source, a work of public art by the Spanish sculptor Jaume Plensa, installed at
the new Bonaventure entrance to the city in the south of the Island of Montreal,
as part of the city's 375th anniversary celebrations. The work was given to
Montrealers by André Desmarais and France Chrétien-Desmarais.

With my granddaughter Jacqueline; my daughter, France; my wife, Aline; my son Hubert; my grandson Olivier; and my son-in-law, André Desmarais; at the unveiling of my official portrait, May 25, 2010, in Ottawa. The painting is an original work by Christan Nicholson.

◀ At Saint James's Palace, very proud to be accompanied by my granddaughter Jacqueline Desmarais de Croÿ-Roeulx.

At a dinner honouring Chief Justice of the Supreme Court Beverley McLachlin on her retirement, with Prime Minister Justin Trudeau and former Prime Minister Brian Mulroney, December 14, 2017.

39

ON THE NEED FOR ART IN LIFE

On Thursday, September 7, 2017, I felt great pride when I saw in *La Presse+* (the digital edition of the Montreal newspaper) a photo of the superb sculpture, thirty-three feet high, that greets people arriving in Montreal along the Bonaventure Expressway. It was the gift of philanthropists I know well: my daughter, France Chrétien Desmarais, and my son-in-law, André Desmarais. This magnificent work, called *Source*, by the distinguished Spanish sculptor Jaume Plensa, was indeed a source of both surprise and pride for Montrealers, giving them a glimpse of their city's beauty and future through the jungle of orange cones they have had to tolerate for so long. Art, in all its forms, makes a huge difference to the life of a community: it lends it a soul. The leaders of cities, provinces, and countries hesitate to invest in such projects, often a bit more costly when they are very beautiful, and that is a serious mistake.

As for us, after having succeeded in balancing the budget, our more generously financed programs permitted us to see the Four Seasons Centre, the new opera house in Toronto, the expansion of the Art Gallery of Ontario by the famous architect Frank Gehry, and the impressive Canadian Museum for Human Rights in Winnipeg. I was particularly interested in the Canadian War Museum in Ottawa, built under my administration, which has become the museum most visited in the capital, even if some see its architecture as being too modern, and even if the military would prefer it to be closer to the Canada Aviation and Space Museum in Rockcliffe. I also intervened, unusually for a prime minister, in another cultural dossier, when the city of Shawinigan transformed the former Alcan factory into vast showrooms where the director of the National Gallery, Pierre Théberge, and the amazing Robert Trudel, director of the Cité de l'Énergie, organized huge sculpture exhibitions every summer—until the Conservatives put an end to this National Gallery program.

During the summer of 2002, they mounted, in these large spaces, a spectacular sculpture exhibition that attracted 65,000 visitors in two and a half months. They borrowed from the artist Louise Bourgeois her immense work called *Maman*, nicknamed "The Spider." It is now standing in front of the National Gallery on Sussex Street in Ottawa, and it is certainly the most photographed work of art in the national capital. I pass by it twice a day, and I always see tourists taking pictures of it. During the summer of 2002 I visited the exhibition in the Shawinigan space along with President Jacques Chirac and his wife, Bernadette. Mme Chirac was struck by this spectacular sculpture and asked me where it came from. I told her that we had borrowed it from Louise Bourgeois, a French artist living in New York. She said, "Jean, if I were prime minister of Canada, I wouldn't send it back to the United States, I would acquire it."

She persuaded me, and when I returned to Ottawa, I summoned the director of the National Gallery, the excellent Pierre Théberge, and I told him to buy the Louise Bourgeois. Like every good civil servant, he told me that he didn't have the necessary budget for such an acquisition. I told him to inform the Treasury Board that he had received an order from the prime minister decreeing that this famous sculpture would never return to New York. When I think of the meaning of this spectacular artwork, I am even happier with what I did. Louise Bourgeois called it *Maman* in honour of her mother, who spent her life repairing ancient tapestries, working from morning to night with patience and dexterity to preserve works of art for generations to come, like a spider tirelessly weaving its web.

Every time a young person asks me what he or she must do to succeed in life, I always reply that the surest way is to work hard. The presence of this symbol representing the idea of work in front of the National Gallery on Sussex Drive, where the country's prime minister resides, is a reminder to whoever has the honour of assuming this great responsibility that he or she must always work very hard.

I have always loved the arts, and I have in fact, over time, put together a collection of Inuit sculptures and drawings. Sometimes I smile when I think that one day I defended before a House of Commons committee the purchase of a painting by Mark Rothko, costing a million dollars. The committee objected: How irresponsible! What a waste of money! etc. Today this canvas is worth thirty million dollars.

Sometimes, music can also be useful in politics. For instance, my minister of intergovernmental affairs, Stéphane Dion, organized in October of 1999 a big conference, at Mont Tremblant, on the subject of federalism. We were receiving delegations from thirty or so countries, and Stéphane wanted the conference to open and close with prestigious guests. He came to see me to say that he wanted the president of the United States, Bill Clinton, to open the conference, and the president of Mexico, Ernesto Zedillo, to be its closing guest. I replied that his request was a bit too ambitious; that it wasn't possible; that the two heads of state had other things to do besides opening or closing conferences.

He insisted and insisted, and I kept repeating that it was impossible. Still, by happy coincidence, Clinton had to come to Ottawa to inaugurate the new American embassy on Sussex Drive. I took advantage of the opportunity, and proposed that he make a speech at the lunch hour at Mont-Tremblant and then play golf with me in the afternoon. He just said, "Great idea, Jean." So I succeeded in my first miracle, and I then called Zedillo in Mexico to ask him to come and close the conference. Unsurprisingly, he told me that it was impossible, because the president of Mexico had to ask his parliament's permission to leave the country. I told him that it was too bad, because if he had accepted my invitation,

Diana Krall would have given him a private performance. You have to know that during a visit to Mexico, Aline and I had had the pleasure of spending a few hours with Zedillo at the presidential palace. For background music the Mexican president had put on a record of Diana Krall's and confessed how much he loved listening to this "white Canadian who sings like an African-American. . . ."

Well, he finally requested and obtained the Mexican parliament's permission to come to Canada. And so Aline and I received Zedillo at 24 Sussex, along with some friends. Diana Krall graciously consented to come and play. I sat Ernesto near the piano, and Diana politely asked him what piece he wanted to hear. The Mexican president was in seventh heaven, and so I had achieved my second miracle. The conference had the president of the United States for its opening, and the president of Mexico for its grand finale. Stéphane Dion thought it was all par for the course, but I was amazed to have brought it off. The arts, music in particular, succeeded in attracting a Mexican president, where the political context would not have sufficed—some would say this was a master stroke.

As I have always believed that the arts contribute in a very important way to a country's quality of life, as soon as we had freed up the budgetary surpluses in 1997, we made our first supplementary allocation to the Department of Canadian Heritage. Also, the first senator we named, Jean-Louis Roux, was one of Canada's great men of the theatre. He ended his career as the chairman of the Canada Council. While I was prime minister, other well-known artists also followed him to the Senate, including Tommy Banks of Alberta, Viola Léger ("La Sagouine") of New Brunswick, and Jean Lapointe of Quebec.

40

ALLAN J. MACEACHEN, A POLITICAL GIANT

I n September 2017 I went to Nova Scotia to attend the memorial for Allan J. MacEachen at the St. Francis Xavier University in Antigonish, Nova Scotia. Allan J. had left us at the age of ninety-six. He was one of the mythic personalities deeply rooted in the historical fabric of the Liberal Party over the 150 years of its existence. He represented, in large part, the "institutional memory" not only of the Liberal Party, but also of the government of Canada, having been an MP for such a long time. He was one of those people who have worked all their lives close to the centre of power, and who could remind us, on occasion, of what our predecessors had done under similar circumstances.

The tributes to this outsize political personage were extraordinary, and worthy of the man. He worked on Parliament Hill for forty-three years, first as an MP, then as senior adviser to the leader of the opposition L.B. Pearson, and finally as a

minister who was a mainstay in the cabinets of prime ministers Pearson and Trudeau between 1963 and 1984. What
talent, and what experience! As cabinet colleagues for eighteen years, we supported each other on major issues and
developed a deep friendship. For him, as for me, our electoral
riding was a top priority, because we knew that without a
seat in Parliament it would be the end of our political careers.
That is why, when I became minister of Indian Affairs and
Northern Development, and so responsible for Parks Canada,
he immediately invited me to his riding to visit the Cape
Breton Highlands National Park, the fortress of Louisbourg,
and the Acadian regions of Chéticamp and Isle Madame. In
the course of this visit, he explained to me the economic
importance of national parks and gave me the idea of establishing a similar park in my region of Saint-Maurice, which
I succeeded in doing three years later.

At regular intervals he invited me to his region for fundraising campaigns and, in particular, to visit Acadian villages
such as Arichat, Gros Nez, Petit Nez, Petit-de-Grat. One
evening, as I was campaigning at Isle Madame, I was
informed that I was the first francophone minister since
Sir Wilfrid Laurier to visit the place and make a speech.
My visits to Cape Breton were among the most wonderful
experiences of my political life. Allan J. and I were great
advocates of regional development. The federal investments
from the 1970s to the present day produced the hoped-for
results. Today the average income of the eastern provinces

represents 90 percent of the average income for Ontario, while before these programs it was only about 50 percent. Signs such as "Now Hiring" were not seen back then.

During a cabinet ministerial retreat at the Keltic Lodge in Ingonish, Allan J. organized a cocktail party so his supporters could meet Prime Minister Trudeau and his ministers. The voters from Bay St. Lawrence reproached me because I had often visited Chéticamp but had never been to their fishing village. And so the next night I made the trip to the village in question, which was in the far northeast of Cape Breton. They gave me a reception I will never forget. With their natural zest for life, these isolated fishers, jolly fellows, fed Canada's justice minister lobster caught out of season, hence illegal, moose meat, also of course out of season, and home-brew. Not bad for a justice minister. . . . While we were eating, a television station was broadcasting a World Series baseball game, and everyone had an eye on it. Suddenly a torrential rain poured down on the village, and the power went out. The game was being hotly contested, and the sports fans were very disappointed. Someone came up with a battery-operated radio and tuned in a station to catch the rest of the game. But the only radio station he found was describing the game in French from the Îles de la Madeleine. And so the minister of justice instantly became a sports commentator, as I was the only francophone in the room who could understand, and describe in English what was going on in the World Series game.

Perhaps the most important episode I lived through with Allan J. was the defeat in the House of Commons of Joe Clark's government on December 13, 1979. Elected at the end of spring that same year, the Conservatives waited until November before presenting their first budget. As Pierre Elliott Trudeau had just announced his retirement, the Liberals found themselves without a leader. Finance Minister John Crosbie was not afraid of having his government defeated by the leaderless Liberals, and decided to present a rather harsh budget, with a substantial hike in the gas tax. As I was the former finance minister, I attended the new minister's closed-door information meeting, just before the budget was presented. The officials made their presentation in English only, and as no one could translate it into French for the Social Credit leader Fabien Roy, who spoke no English, I, out of necessity, became his translator. I knew that Social Credit was thinking of supporting the Crosbie budget, but I think my French interpretation persuaded Fabien to abstain from voting rather than to back it.

I told Allan J. that with the anticipated abstention of Social Credit, we could defeat the Clark government if all our members voted. As the opposition leader in the House, Allan J. informed Trudeau of what was happening. Trudeau replied that he was going to think things over before deciding to bring down the government. He added that if he did not call back before five o'clock, Allan could take the necessary measures to defeat the government. At half past four I went to Allan's office to await Trudeau's final decision. The fateful hour came, and there was no call from our leader. We both got up, a bit nervous, shook hands, and wished each other luck for the election to come. When it came time to vote, all the Liberals were in their seats, even the member from Trois-Rivières, who came out of the hospital to join in the vote with his colleagues. Roger Simmons, who had been elected in a by-election a few days earlier and had been sworn in that morning, voted with us that same evening. He had only sat for one day during that session. The briefing I had given that day produced the desired result, because the abstention of Fabien Roy's Social Credit Party led to a rejection of my friend John Crosbie's budget. As a result, Prime Minister Joe Clark had to call an election, which he lost.

This Conservative defeat, in my opinion, had a profound impact. Trudeau, who had been leader of the Liberal Party during four elections, did not want to face a confidence vote at the biannual meeting of the party, nor did he want to continue in politics. He had decided, sometime in the course of the preceding months, to retire. Meanwhile, René Lévesque had decided to hold a referendum in May 1980. When he made that decision, he was very happy to be facing a Joe Clark rather than a Pierre Elliott Trudeau as prime minister of Canada. But on the fateful day of Joe Clark's defeat, Trudeau saw that this would be an opportunity for him to become Liberal leader and prime minister again, in order to confront René Lévesque's separatists. And history proved him right.

And so Allan J. MacEachen and Jean Chrétien remained grateful to Fabien Roy for his willingness to change his position on the basis of an interpretation of the budget rendered necessary by his unilingualism.

41

HUMOUR AS A POLITICAL WEAPON

In this late autumn 2017, when we wake every morning vaguely uneasy about what's been done during the night by our two daddy's boys, Donald Trump, president of the United States, and Kim Jong-un, leader of North Korea, with their power to provoke a nuclear disaster, an urge to laugh does not often enter our minds. There was a time when politicians, despite their day-to-day concerns, loved to laugh and even used humour to achieve their goals. Of course, that was a time when political correctness was not an obsession. You could still laugh, almost without giving it a second thought. That's why what follows may at times seem a bit farcical, though it may persuade you that politics could be more civilized than it is today.

In my case, a good dose of humour has often served as an effective political weapon. The naked truth is sometimes hard to swallow, but when it is deftly overlaid with humour, it goes down much more easily. My region, the Mauricie valley, produced at least three successful politicians with a real gift throughout their careers for wielding humour. They were Maurice Duplessis, Réal Caouette, and Camille Samson. They certainly inspired me, and maybe I inherited some of their skill at presenting complex political issues with down-to-earth humour close to the people and their daily lives. Their humour, like my own, has often been looked down upon in certain circles, where it's not considered sophisticated enough. However that may be, this down-home humour has often shown itself to be very effective, whatever the killjoys may say, and I applied it with a certain success during my forty years of public life. Here are a few gems that marked the success of those three exceptional politicians from my part of the world.

During the 1949 provincial election, Duplessis was put on the defensive by his Liberal opponents from the very outset over the problem of rural electrification. In his first campaign speech, the old fox began by saying, "Électeurs, électrices, électricité!" With one well-placed word, "électricité," Duplessis had disarmed the bomb. Bachelor that he was, he liked to say that he was married to the province. Given his name, Maurice le Noblet Duplessis, he was criticized for being a bit too bourgeois, so he kept two hats in his car: a new one, clean and fashionable, for his bourgeois outings, and one that was battered and shabby for meeting the people. His humour could often be extremely caustic. Talking, for example, about a lawyer whom he had just named to the provincial court, he said of him, "I did not name him judge, I created a judge, because I made a judge from nothing."

Another time, while attending a reception where Jean Bruchési was also present, a former ambassador who became a senior official in Quebec, Duplessis heard him say that his name should not be pronounced "Bruchési," but rather "Brukési." Maurice immediately shot back, laughing, "M. Brukési, you make me 'kier,'" an untranslatable pun linking his name to an undignified bodily function.

The first leader of the Créditistes, Quebec's Social Credit Party, Réal Caouette, was born in what is today Shawinigan. Many members of his family were friends of my father, and when I shook his hand in the House of Commons, he told me, laughing, "You're not the one who beat my candidate, it's your father." I sometimes sat down with him in the House of Commons, and one day he confessed that his family was very Liberal, and that when all the family members recited the rosary in the living room after supper, kneeling before the crucifix and a portrait of Sir Wilfrid Laurier, they didn't know which of the two they were praying to.

Immediately after he was elected leader of the Liberal Party of Canada and sworn in as prime minister, Pierre Elliott Trudeau called a general election. Trudeaumania broke out in English Canada, but not in Quebec. In fact, we lost five seats in Quebec, and Caouette picked up five more, largely thanks to his passion and his humour. As minister of justice, Trudeau had passed his omnibus bill, among other things decriminalizing homosexuality, and declaring that the government had no business in the bedrooms of the nation. In the televised leaders' debate that followed, Réal was asked what he thought about the legalization of homosexuality. He replied that he had no problem with it, except, he said: "How are we going to educate their children?" This remark, totally out of place in today's context, elicited roars of laughter in the rural Quebec of the time.

While my own electoral campaign made my entry into the cabinet at the age of only thirty-three a key argument in favour of my candidacy, Caouette, in a single sentence, demolished it with a rather crude slogan that his supporters freely used against me: "Minister or no minister, no caprice in Saint-Maurice, we vote Créditiste, *câlisse!*" (A popular religious profanity.) Not very sophisticated, but effective enough that my majority went from 7,000 votes to barely 2,000. How can you fight that?

Finally, the third of these exceptional politicians, Camille Samson, was born in the same neighbourhood as me; he was also a classmate of Aline's in elementary school, and later became leader of the provincial Social Credit Party. At the end of his career, when I was prime minister, he joined my team, and we became good friends. When he was a Social Credit member in the National Assembly, he had the reputation of being the most colourful person there. It was he who represented his party on the No committee during the 1980 referendum. For weeks, Claude Ryan, the chair of the No committee, Camille Samson, Michelle Tisseyre, and I appeared together at public meetings.

Camille was always very funny, and here are three of his quips to prove it. He liked to say that you had to really believe in Canada to be in favour of the No side, because he lived in Rouyn-Noranda, right next to Ontario, while his mother-in-law lived in Sudbury, Ontario, and if Quebec separated she would need a passport to come and visit him.

He also said he found the 103-word question posed by the separatists so confusing that it was as if René Lévesque were telling the Québécois to jump from the top of Place Ville Marie, and if by the tenth floor they weren't happy, he'd pass a bill to amend the law of gravity!!!

In all public consultations during the weeks preceding a vote, there are fluctuations in the polls. The 1980 referendum was no exception. Camille Samson had fun with this phenomenon, saying that he did his own polling, and at the start of the campaign, he'd gone down into his basement where his cat had given birth to nine kittens. He asked them how they intended to vote in the referendum, and the nine kittens said that they would vote Yes. Four weeks later he went back down to the basement to ask the same question, and this time the nine kittens replied that they would vote No. He then asked the meeting: "Do you know why they changed their minds? It's because now their eyes were open."

You can see that sometimes humour in politics can first make you smile, and then make you think.

42

MEMORIES FROM MAJOR INTERNATIONAL CONFERENCES

The major international meetings of heads of state and government leaders often lead to bizarre situations and exchanges. For example, during the NATO summit in Madrid in July 1997, Bill Clinton, who had the bad habit of arriving more than an hour late, did so at a reception given by the King of Spain. The night before, and in the morning for a special breakfast, he was also late, and you could feel the mounting frustration among the leaders. And so to lighten the atmosphere, I launched into a humorous tirade on American governance, including the powers of the president, so restricted by the Senate and Congress that a presidential "yes" was not a yes but a maybe; on the Republicans of the North, who were closer to the Democrats of the North than the Republicans of the South, and vice versa; on the fact that there was really no political party, because the president had no control over the nomination of his party's candidates. And so forth.

When I took my place at the conference table, my neighbour, Prime Minister Jean-Luc Dehaene of Belgium, who had missed my humorous presentation, asked me to repeat it. And so I repeated in French what I'd said in English to our colleagues. Now, the microphone in front of us was open, and several journalists heard my not very diplomatic quips. And there were fireworks. My diplomatic adviser, James Bartleman, wouldn't repeat to me the words that the American national security adviser, Sandy Berger, had uttered about me, for fear of offending my sensitive ears. Our ambassador in Washington, Raymond Chrétien, was given an earful by American authorities, and Bill Clinton found a diplomatic way out by saying that he would get even when we next played golf. I let the storm pass over the next two days, and when I contacted Bill to apologize, he graciously accepted my excuses, and told me that the same thing—speaking into a microphone inadvertently left open—had happened to him and that there was a lot of truth in what I'd said. I'm pretty sure he won our next golf game.

On another occasion, when I was in London for a meeting of the leaders of progressive parties looking for a third way between socialism and liberalism, which was attended by Clinton of the United States, Blair of the United Kingdom, Schroeder of Germany, Cardoso of Brazil, and ten or so other leaders, we allowed one question per country at the press conference. When it was the turn of the Canadian journalist, he asked me a question about the Canadian economy that was not appropriate in the context. A bit frustrated, I replied that the Canadian economy was in very good shape and that we only had one problem: "*one* goddamn mad cow." Clinton began to laugh and laugh and laugh. . . . After the adjournment he told me, "Jean, only you could say 'one goddamn mad cow' in front of the international press and get away with it."

Another time, during a visit to the White House, while Bill Clinton and I were holding a press conference, I said in a moment of enthusiasm that Canada was the best country in the world. Imagine the scene: I'm in the White House Rose Garden beside the president of the United States, and I'm shamelessly lauding the virtues of my country. It was neither the right place nor the right time, but what was said was said. Clinton replied, "Are you sure of that, Jean?" Aware of my gaffe, I just answered, laughing, "Absolutely."

In Naples, during the 1994 G7 summit, for the last lunch we had a meal that was attended by the seven heads of government without their officials, and we wanted to honour François Mitterrand, who was completing his fourteenth and last summit. At a certain point, I said that if Lower Canada had joined the American Revolution, the language of the United States would probably be French, because Louisiana (named in honour of Louis XIV) was an American state,

Jefferson and Adams had both been ambassadors in Paris, and the vote on the matter in Congress would have been very tight between French and English. I could see Mitterrand imagining himself as president of the United States, what a beautiful dream! Bill Clinton then said that if French were the language of his country, he would probably be here taking notes for President Chrétien. It was very kind indeed of him.

Ten years later I had an opportunity to return the kindness. In the spring of 2003, after an official visit to Santo Domingo, I remained to vacation on the island, and played golf with Clinton. At the end of the game, we had lunch at the house of one of his Latin American friends, and I told the guests that Bill Clinton was very popular in Canada. Joking, I said that I had the power to make him an instant citizen of our country. That way, he could run to succeed me as leader of the Liberal Party of Canada, and could be prime minister before the end of the year. Bill burst out laughing, and slapping his thigh, he said, "I know all the files, and I could really take George W. to the cleaners. . . ."

Despite what the right-wing papers had to say on the subject, my personal relations with George W. Bush were very cordial. Like me, he was among the first to arrive at meetings, and that gave us a chance to have some private conversations while waiting for the others. I was the only one who could talk baseball and football with him. On one of those days, talking about baseball, as he had been president and co-owner of the Texas

Rangers baseball team, I reminded him that as president of the Rangers he had signed a contract with Alex Rodriguez for $25 million a year for ten years, for a total of $250 million, and that to earn that much money as president of the United States, at a salary of $500,000, would take him only five hundred years. And to conclude, "What can I say, George, those are today's values."

When the newly elected President George W. Bush came to Quebec in April 2001 for the Summit of the Americas, there was a single, nagging issue dividing our two countries: the United States was not allowing Prince Edward Island potatoes into its country for, it said, reasons of public health. For the three days of his visit, I made sure that Prince Edward Island potatoes were on the menu whenever possible. At the end of the summit, the Three Amigos of NAFTA—the president of the United States, the president of Mexico, and myself—along with our foreign ministers, had a business lunch. When we were seated, Bush looked at the menu, which was written only in French, and turned to Colin Powell so he could tell him what he was going to be eating. Powell told him that once again they would be eating potatoes that were banned in the United States. And so I told President Bush that he and all the other heads of government, and the ministers and officials of the thirty-four countries present, had for three days been savouring the notorious potatoes, and that no one was sick, and so on. Result: a few days later the embargo was lifted. The things I had to do to fulfil my duties as prime minister!

When I met Tony Blair for the first time at the G8 summit in Denver in 1997, I felt instantly at ease with the young, energetic, intelligent, and ambitious politician, who like me loved politics and was proud to be serving. As Great Britain and Canada were members of the Commonwealth and had similar parliamentary systems, we often shared the same views. A short time after he became the prime minister of his country, Tony found himself in trouble at the Commonwealth meeting over which he was presiding in Edinburgh. Some Muslim countries in the Commonwealth wanted us to admit Palestine into our organization, without demanding of it the normal requirements. Suddenly Blair sent me a note asking me to help him. So I said that as prime minister of Canada, I would not agree to the meeting recognizing Quebec as an independent country, and that the prime minister of St. Kitts and Nevis would not like it either if Nevis were declared an independent country, and that to declare Scotland an independent country, even here in Edinburgh, would not make the Scottish member present happy either. That was the end of the discussion, and very kindly Blair came to thank me in French.

I was impressed by what he had done since his election as leader of the Labour party. In a few years he had succeeded in transforming his party, bogged down in the doctrinaire tangles of the left, into a modern party, progressive, reasonable, and, above all, attractive to the electorate. After the long, controversial reign of Margaret Thatcher, he had turned his country into a modern and progressive political beacon. Unfortunately, he made a grave error in committing his country to the war in Iraq, but he did not deserve the unpopularity he experienced after leaving political life. For me, he will remain a great politician with whom I got along very well indeed. In his memoirs, he may have expressed, better than anyone, what bound us together: "I was in Canada to address the Parliament, and meet my friend Jean Chrétien, the Canadian Prime Minister. He was a very wise, wily and experienced old bird, great at international meetings where he could be counted on to talk sense, and, as Canadians often are, firm and dependable without being pushy. All in all, a good guy and a very tough political operator not to be underestimated."

That is what makes me smile when I think of what I said to him (this story too is in his memoirs) when he consulted me over his own problems with mad cow disease: "Watch that, young Tony, watch it very carefully, that's trouble." It's true that I was twenty years older than him, but nevertheless, for the prime minister of a former colony like Canada to call the prime minister of Great Britain "young Tony," even if it made him laugh, was perhaps going a bit far.

43

OUR OFFICIAL LANGUAGES AND ME

A s a young lawyer with a degree from a classical college in rural Quebec, I began to practise my profession in a city that was 95 percent francophone. My command of the language of Shakespeare was very limited when I became a Liberal candidate in 1963. One day we organized a meeting of anglophones in the riding, and in a very short speech in English, I promised them that if I were elected their MP, I would be bilingual by the next election. About fifteen years later, while I was telling the story of that episode to some friends, Prime Minister Trudeau said, jokingly, that I had not yet entirely kept my promise, even if I'd been named Canada's finance minister. My difficulties with the other official language are well known overall, but I'd like to relate a few particularly comical incidents that resulted from them.

Invited to dinner at the home of my colleague Rick Cashin along with several others, all anglophones, I was asked by one of them to explain how I had succeeded, in such a short time, in converting my opponent's nearly 10,000-vote majority into a victory for myself. It was the first time I expressed myself in English before a group of listeners. With great difficulty, I told them that for forty-nine days, from morning to night, I was on the streets, in the stores, and above all at the factory gates, shaking hands. When the men and women came out in too large a number and at times too rapidly, I just touched their arms, or as I put it, "Sometimes I would only touch them on the *bras*." Of course everyone burst out laughing, and someone quipped, "Now we understand why you won the election!"

On another occasion, after a speech in Toronto when I was a young minister, someone asked me who was this influential individual in Quebec, Claude Ryan. I replied that he was the editor of a very important newspaper, *Le Devoir*, which many political figures consulted, and of course that pleased him. He was a serious and impressive man whose very presence lent him an influence comparable to that of a cardinal at the time. And so we were almost inclined to get down on our knees and kiss his ring. Except I used the French word "bague" rather than the appropriate English word "ring," and everyone again burst out laughing. Unfortunately, in the other official language, the word "bag" is used to describe, rather than the apostolic ring, that part of a man's anatomy that I would rather not describe here in detail.

In time, my English greatly improved, but my French accent remained marked. And so I asked my English teacher to help me get rid of it. But Mrs. McDonald told me, "You must at all costs not lose this accent, because whoever hears you on the radio knows right away that it's Minister Jean

Chrétien who is speaking. Coca-Cola would pay a lot to have that kind of recognition." After more than fifty years in Ottawa, this accent still allows me to say, as a joke, "There was only Maurice Chevalier and me who had to practise to keep their French accent in English." (Maurice Chevalier was a French singer and actor who was very popular in the United States during the 1950s and 1960s.)

In September 1977, at the annual meeting in Washington of finance ministers with the directors of the International Monetary Fund and the World Bank, as I was the first francophone to be finance minister, I gave my speech entirely in French, which created a certain stir among the anglophone journalists. For those among them who asked for an explanation, I just told them that for decades Canada spoke only English at these meetings, but as of today everyone knows that there are two official languages in Canada. When I got home, Trudeau congratulated me with a big grin.

During the 1993 federal election, I was campaigning in Eastern Ontario, the most Loyalist part of Canada, which had, among other landmarks, a "Loyalist Boulevard" and a "Loyalist Motel." Coming out of the "Loyalist Legion," a rather corpulent individual stopped me and grabbed me with both arms, saying, "My name is Lamothe, I'm a farmer in this neck of the woods, and I never thought I'd ever see a politician get a standing ovation around here with a speech given partly in French." I replied, "Canada has changed!"

In the spring of 1982 I went to London, as the justice minister responsible for the patriation of the Constitution, to finalize the procedures. I was to be present at the moment when the British Parliament was passing its last law concerning Canada, because Canada was putting an end to its legal link with the Parliament of Great Britain. As protocol required me to inform the Queen, I went to Buckingham Palace for a private meeting with Her Majesty. She knew that this was a historic moment for Canadians. I told her, "When you sign the royal proclamations of the British Parliament, the words preceding your signature are 'La Reine le veult.' And so, Your Majesty, may I have the pleasure of making my presentation to you in my mother tongue? That would be very meaningful to me." The Queen graciously acceded to my request, and for this historic encounter we used the language of Molière.

For someone who spoke hardly any English when he became an MP twenty years earlier, after an election in a riding where 95 percent of the citizens were francophones, this gave me much pleasure and a great deal of pride.

I might add that if the Queen enjoyed speaking French with Aline and me, as did Prince Philip for that matter, it was perhaps because when we met the Queen Mother, she rushed up to us to take advantage of the opportunity to speak French. One day she told me that she had begun speaking English at the age of five. Until then she had spoken only French, as her father, a great francophile, had entrusted her to French nannies till then. Surprising, n'est-ce pas?

During my entire career, I made it my duty to speak both official languages, and I must say that I appreciated the fact that Stephen Harper did so as well. At a G8 meeting, Paul Martin was reproached by President Chirac for never speaking French, and one day when Paul did decide to speak the language, Chirac, mischievously, called on an interpreter, just to tease him a little.

And so you will understand that when I think about everything that has happened to me during my long career, one of my greatest satisfactions is that I was able to persuade Prime Minister Pierre Trudeau, and then the anglophone provincial premiers, to inscribe in the Canadian Charter of Rights and Freedoms the right for all Canadians to be educated in one of the country's two official languages.

Trudeau had promised that the patriation of the Constitution and the inclusion of the Charter of Rights and Freedoms would not change the balance of power between the federal government and the provinces. That was why he had decided he would not touch education.

When I had finished my work with the provinces and the parliamentary committees and was completing my progress report for the prime minister, he congratulated me on a job well done. Nonetheless, I told him, I was still sorry I hadn't been able to persuade him to include in the Charter of Rights and Freedoms the right to education in the two official languages. I explained to him that in 1907, the Boisverts, who represented the maternal branch of my family, left Quebec to homestead in St. Paul, Alberta, and that most of them had to all intents and purposes lost their language because there was no French school in the province. Now, when a unique opportunity presented itself to correct that situation, I had failed at the task. After a long silence, he said to me, "Jean, do it!" and I replied, "Thank you, Pierre." What an extraordinary moment, unforgettable, and critical for the future of francophones and of our country!

44

THE JUDICIARY: LONG LIVE THE CANADIAN SYSTEM!

Last night, December 14, 2017, a thousand admirers, among them the governor general, the prime minister, several former prime ministers and governors general, cabinet ministers, judges, lawyers, and other distinguished citizens, crowded into the Shaw Centre in Ottawa to pay homage to the chief justice of the Supreme Court of Canada, Beverley McLachlin, who was retiring after serving for eighteen years in a post of crucial importance to the proper functioning of Canadian institutions and our democracy.

It was a magnificent evening of tributes to an exceptional woman, born in a small Alberta town, who climbed the ladder of Canadian society rung by rung to become the first woman to attain the highest level of the judiciary, thanks to her intelligence, her hard work, her tenacity, her charm, and her pride in being Canadian. But beyond all these qualities, it was the acuteness and the sensitivity of her judgments that inspired confidence in Canadians and in due course took her to the heights.

For this unique individual, perfectly bilingual, the wife of a true gentleman, tributes came from all over Canada, and notably, from the chief justices of dozens of countries on every continent.

Of course, I felt especially proud because in 1981, when I was minister of justice, I had named her to the Supreme Court of British Columbia. And at the turn of the third millennium in 2000, this time as prime minister, I had the great privilege of appointing her to be the first woman to serve as chief justice of the Supreme Court of Canada. I like to see it as a heralding of the rise of women, slow in certain instances perhaps but inexorable, to the highest positions of our society. In 1989 my predecessor, Brian Mulroney, named Beverley McLachlin to the Supreme Court of Canada, making her the second woman to be elevated to that court. The first was Bertha Wilson, whom Prime Minister Pierre Elliott Trudeau had named in 1982, on my recommendation as minister of justice.

We were both present that evening of December 2017—Brian Mulroney, the Conservative, and me, the Liberal—and happy to be at the celebration, neither of us knowing if Beverley McLachlin had ever in her life expressed a political preference for one party or another. What a contrast to what is happening among our neighbours to the south, where the nomination of a judge to the Supreme Court involves a never-ending partisan debate concerning the individual's personal life, family, business, educational history, his or her beliefs, and any possible biases, while judges are in principle named simply to interpret the laws passed by the country's lawmakers and those of each of the American states.

Here in Canada we are privileged to have the least politicized judiciary that I know. All those who aspire to become judges see their competence analyzed by officials specialized in the field, then screened by the provincial and the Canadian Bar, with the participation of the chief justices of the courts concerned, while very often the attorneys general of the provinces also have their say.

Working from an approved list, the minister of justice recommends a nomination to the cabinet and to the prime minister. In such a system, at the end of the line it's the reputations of the minister of justice and the government that are at stake. If a nomination proves disastrous, they are held responsible. The corridors of the law courts, filled with lawyers who rub shoulders with judges every day, become the people's tribunes for the decision, and if the nominations are bad, the reputations of the justice minister and the government suffer. Whence the need to be vigilant.

As prime minister, and as a minister who had practised law before entering politics, I have had the opportunity to participate in the nominations of hundreds of judges to the Supreme Court, the Federal Court, and the Superior Courts of the provinces, without ever having been the object of critical personal attacks. Of course, I have often been solicited by friends, supporters, and other aspirants. And of course I've supported many candidates, but I've also refused to support others whom I've considered simply unqualified. I took very seriously the responsibility of making these selections, because I was aware of the exceptional quality of our judiciary system, and I knew that for a society to function well, it is essential to have a legal system that is stable, independent, professional and, above all, respected by public opinion. In short, a system in which the citizens have confidence, and that is precisely what we have here in Canada.

During the celebration of the highly respected Beverley McLachlin, who has left such a mark on the history of the Canadian judiciary, the ex–chief justice of the Supreme Court of Canada found herself surrounded by two political adversaries: the former Conservative prime minister Brian Mulroney, and the former Liberal prime minister Jean Chrétien, both lawyers from the Quebec Bar, one having exercised his profession in the big city, the other in a provincial town. Two former heads of government who had participated in the rise of an exceptional jurist, a woman born in a small Western Canadian town who rose to the most important position in our legal system. This image carries with it the symbolic charge of a society that knows how to achieve a consensus beyond partisan debate. This symbol embodies, in my opinion, the exceptional quality of our country's political institutions. When we compare our institutions to those of our southern neighbour, I have no problem in proclaiming once again, "Vive le Canada! Long live Canada!"

Postscript: In order not to spoil the mood of the moment, and out of generosity, I have decided to deliberately ignore the unacceptable attitude of former prime minister Harper regarding the Supreme Court of Canada, and in particular its chief justice. It was nothing less than an utterly unprecedented violation of the tradition honoured by Canadians, of respect for this fundamental institution. Let us just call it an aberrant moment in our country's history.

45

CANADA, THE ENVY OF THE WORLD

In Spain, an election was held recently in the province of Catalonia, in the midst of a constitutional crisis. The three parties in favour of separation won a small majority of seats, but the parties supporting unity with Spain garnered more votes, and the party that won the largest number of seats opposes Catalonia's separation. Madrid continues to talk about the rule of law and repeats that legally, no province can separate from the country. No country in the European Union supports Catalonia's separatist movement. What a mess! It's a situation that's quite familiar to someone like me, who was the minister responsible for the 1980 referendum for the federal government, and prime minister of the country during the 1995 referendum.

The Spanish government's assertion of the country's indivisibility is in no way revolutionary. On the contrary. For example, the French constitution and that of the United States make the same affirmation. In fact, the Americans went to war to prevent the Southern states from seceding.

What is more, international law decrees that a province cannot issue a unilateral declaration of independence unless that province is a colony, or basic rights and personal freedoms are being systematically violated. This is certainly not the case in Catalonia, Quebec, or Scotland.

That is what the Supreme Court of Canada recognized in 1998 at the time of the appeal regarding the secession of Quebec, when it had to decide whether a province had the right to unilaterally separate from Canada following a referendum. In 1980, during a meeting of Pierre Elliott Trudeau's cabinet, discussion on the stance that the federal government ought to take in the event of a referendum on the separation of Quebec was extremely heated, fascinating, and definitely historic. On one side were those who maintained that Canada was indivisible because the Fathers of Confederation had not foreseen this possibility, and that when the premier of Nova Scotia, Joseph Howe, threatened to pull his province out of Canada in 1869, no one really took him seriously. Those who were against separation also asserted that according to international law, Quebec would not meet the legal conditions for a unilateral proclamation of independence. In short, they proclaimed that Canada was indivisible, and that we just had to face facts and admit that an independent Quebec could not be envisaged. That was the position of those who argued for the impossibility of separation, whom I would call the "legalists."

On the other side were what I would call the "democrats," who claimed that Canada was the voluntary gathering together of former English colonies that had united: first Lower and Upper Canada, Nova Scotia, and New Brunswick, then Prince Edward Island, followed by British Columbia, and finally, almost a hundred years later, Newfoundland, which also voluntarily joined Confederation. From this point of view, as the provinces had of their own free will joined Canada, they could also decide to leave the confederation, following a democratic process. They had joined Canada according to certain prior conditions. They could also leave under certain conditions, while taking a democratic approach.

I would say that most of the cabinet ministers opposed recognizing a formula consisting of conditions, referendum, and separation. Prime Minister Trudeau settled the bitter debate in favour of the "democrats"; that is to say, he permitted a referendum in Quebec, expressing his conviction that most Québécois would vote in favour of the bond with Canada. He had not foreseen that the Parti Québécois government would pose ambiguous questions; that the words "separation" or "separatist" would be replaced by the new words "indépendantiste" and "souverainiste." Words that the *Petit Robert*, the French dictionary, only recognized in 1969, for "indépendantiste," and in 1976, for "souverainiste." Moreover, the first time the word "indépendantiste" appeared in the *Petit Robert* in 1969, the definition given was "Quebec separatist."

In retrospect, I realize that holding a referendum is not without consequences. Catalonia is losing dozens of businesses that are leaving to set up shop elsewhere. It was the same thing in Quebec after the victory of the Parti Québécois in 1976, and one of my greatest political frustrations came in 1978, when I was Canada's finance minister. Montreal, which in the 1960s was Canada's greatest metropolis, lost this role to Toronto. Perhaps Bay Street ought to erect a monument to thank the Parti Québécois. One of the most painful memories of my career was of a meeting with the president of Sun Life, at which I tried to persuade him not to move his head office from Montreal to Toronto. He and his family had already left Quebec, and Sun Life was going to do the same, end of story. It didn't matter if I said that if his company still existed, it was because the federal government had passed legislation to forestall a takeover of his insurance company by a larger one in New York. He didn't budge. I had him meet with Prime Minister Trudeau, but again, no success. His self-importance, arrogance, and intransigence was stunning. And the narrowness of this man's mind really made me lose my temper, a rare occurrence. The federal government had saved his company, but he wouldn't lift a finger to save the country.

Most often, those who are for separation are guided by their hearts and their emotions, while those who are against it are guided by reason. That is what makes it hard for the partisans of national unity to declaim from a rostrum. It's easier to talk about the thirty-minute Battle of the Plains of Abraham and to mourn the death of Montcalm than to explain that we in fact became British subjects only in 1763, with the signing of the Treaty of Paris. It was only after a war that lasted seven years that Louis XV had to cede New France, whose territory extended from Quebec to Louisiana, after France's overall defeat in Europe at the hands of Great Britain.

But what is most difficult in a referendum is that emotions reach such a pitch that families are split, friendships die, villages divide, and often even people who are ordinarily fair and reasonable become aggressive, belligerent, hateful, and sometimes frankly insulting. I have of course been a victim of that on a number of occasions, and have found myself responding in kind. I had uncivilized exchanges with René Lévesque and others, which I dare not put into writing. Emotions become so extreme that you feel as though you are crushing the dearest dream of reasonable adults. There was, for instance, in my riding, a separatist politician with whom I had an excellent personal relationship. As a student I had worked with his father at a paper mill, and I had fond memories of that time. One day, I asked this member of the National Assembly how his father was. He replied that he had died not long before, and that on his deathbed he had confessed that he would die unhappy because Quebec had not become an independent country. Truly, to destroy a child's illusion is already unfortunate, but to shatter the long-held dream of an adult is infinitely more painful. All this is most regrettable.

The referendum is a democratic instrument that is hard to handle, and it rarely produces appropriate solutions. The questions are often poorly expressed or deliberately deceptive. Who remembers the two questions, or even one, posed by the 1980 and 1995 referendums? In the end, international law does not allow for the unilateral proclamation of independence. The English voted yes on Brexit for the wrong reasons, and are now locked into a position with consequences that are much more weighty and unforeseeable than those anticipated at the time of the consultation. The Catalans voted yes in a referendum that was boycotted by the majority and are certainly not out of the woods. For myself, I could write some very long chapters on the two referendums in which I had to play an important role. All I ask of my successors, my fellow citizens in Quebec, and the rest of Canada is this: for the love of God, do not follow again those paths that pit us against one another, disregarding everything that we have in common. Compared with other countries, Canada's problems are benign. We are extremely privileged, and in almost every domain, we are the envy of the world. Even if it is thirty degrees below zero on this last day of 2017, Canada is still "the *most best* country in the world." So there!

46

POTPOURRI

N ow I'm setting down on paper some anecdotes I tell now and then, a mixed bag of memories that I'd like to share with you. For instance, consider Jean Marchand when he left the cabinet to accept his friend Pierre Elliott Trudeau's offer to sit in the Senate. To be able to represent Quebec, each senator must own a property, worth at least $4,000, in the riding he represents. This requirement does not exist in the other provinces, which proves that Quebec is a distinct society. And so Jean went off one day in search of a piece of land to buy in his riding, and found a farmer who offered him some property for $2,500. Marchand asked, "Would you accept $4,000?" The deal was done, and Jean qualified to become a senator. This sum of $4,000 has not changed since 1967.

Jean Lapierre was elected as an MP in 1979, just a few days after turning twenty-three, and when he left the federal parliament in 1992 at the age of thirty-six, after only thirteen years of service, he became eligible for a lifetime pension that would seem very generous to any ordinary mortal. Preston Manning's populist Reform Party decided to capitalize on this very rare situation during the 1993 election campaign in order to heap blame on Brian Mulroney's Conservatives. They promised to abolish the pension plan for MPs. To highlight this position, Deborah Grey, a fine MP from Alberta, arrived on Parliament Hill with a pig in her arms on the day the bill my government had introduced to correct the situation was being studied.

The afternoon of the vote, all the Reform members wore a badge with a picture of a pig crossed out with a big X. When the government members began to stand up to vote, one after the other, the Reformists started to make a noise that was supposed to represent an angry pig. It was then that Doug Young, the jovial minister of national defence, cried out, "I didn't know you were bilingual." As few of the Reformists spoke the language of Molière, there was general laughter. Aline, who was at home watching it all on television, told me that she heard me laughing louder than the others. As was the case every time we voted on salary increases, some members voted against but then accepted the increase with pleasure. This time, to lay a trap for the Reformists, we inserted a measure stipulating that a member wanting to receive a pension even if he had voted against it would have to sign an official request before the Clerk of the House of Commons. All the Reformists did so, except for their leader, Preston Manning.

People of conviction, really?

———

Well now, was my friend the minister of agriculture Eugene Whelan really in trouble when I heard the opposition, all scandalized, accuse him of travelling to Miami in a government airplane? In response, "Gino," as we called him, got up in the House looking embarrassed and contrite, to admit that it really was true, he'd taken the government plane and had indeed gone to Miami using transportation paid for by taxpayers. But the purpose of his trip was to meet Canadian farmers in Miami, Miami Canadians. . . . After a long pause, he added that the officials had just omitted to mention that the destination was Miami, Manitoba, and not Florida!

In 2000, shortly after becoming president of Russia, Vladimir Putin paid a visit to his neighbour to the north, Canada. After a lavish dinner in the magnificent dining room of the National Gallery, I proposed to walk with him and his entourage to the Château Laurier, a few hundred metres down the road. On the way, we went into the Earl of Sussex Tavern and had a beer along with the clients who were very surprised to be lifting a glass alongside the Russian president and the Canadian prime minister. After a short pause, we continued our walk along Sussex Street in the direction of the Château. Passing in front of the Department of National Revenue, a Russian member of the delegation asked why he had seen more than twenty prostitutes on the sidewalk at ten in the morning, and yet there were none at ten o'clock at night. We had to inform him that here, the sidewalk served as a smoking room for the employees, since it was forbidden to smoke inside, and that no transactions were being made!

The day after being named to the Senate, Raymond Setlakwe went with his wife, Yvette, to the dentist. While his wife was receiving professional care, Senator Raymond, alone in the waiting room, fell asleep in his chair. When the treatment was over, the doctor and Yvette surprised him in that state. The dentist said to Yvette, "Your husband works too hard, and I can see that he's very tired." Yvette, who has a good sense of humour, replied, "It's not exhaustion, doctor, he's practising for his new job in the Senate!"

In 1978, my nephew Raymond Chrétien, then only thirty-six years old, was named ambassador to Zaïre, now the Democratic Republic of Congo (the DRC), whose controversial president at the time was Mobutu Sese Seko. And so I began to take a special interest in that African country, and to follow its progress. When I was in New York in the autumn of 2001 to give a speech at the General Assembly of the United Nations, I asked to meet the brand new president of the DRC, Joseph Kabila, barely thirty years old, who had just replaced his father Laurent-Désiré Kabila, who had been assassinated the preceding January.

The officials organized a meeting, but when I arrived, instead of seeing a thirty-year-old president, I saw a president my own age. It was not President Kabila of the Belgian Congo, but rather President Denis Sassou-Nguesso of the French Congo. Our official had got the wrong Congo. I realized the error immediately, but I acted as though everything was normal. The president of this very small country was surprised and honoured that a G7 member had asked to see him. The meeting went well, and he took the opportunity to ask me for help with some visa problems, including one for a member of his family who needed special medical care.

The president of the Republic of Congo (and *not* the Democratic Republic of Congo: an understandable confusion) never learned about the error. The official who made the gaffe wanted to die and so did I, but, as we say, we laughed instead.

Like millions of Canadians during the winter freeze, Aline and I like to spend a few days in the South. Even if I had invitations from MPs, ministers, friends, and businessmen, I preferred to go to the summer home of my daughter and son-in-law in Florida. The house was built beside a magnificent golf course, and very near the sea. Often, when Aline and I played golf, our favourite sport, we invited the American bodyguards to play along with us.

At the end of our vacation, traditionally, I often gave them golf balls as souvenirs, with a maple leaf and my signature printed on each one. These balls were paid for by my riding's Liberal association to be given away as souvenirs to those who participated in our annual golf tournament, and my staff saved what was left over for my own use. Now, at a certain point we had no more, and without informing me, my office took the initiative of buying some. They bought nine hundred dollars' worth of golf balls. The Gomery Commission team brought this to light before the start of their hearings. Scandal! The prime minister uses golf balls paid for by the state!!! Outside the hearing rooms, Judge Gomery was even heard to say that this was "small-town cheap."

When I appeared before the commission to testify, I decided to reply in kind, and I brought along some golf balls that I'd received as gifts. The first ones that I pulled out of my briefcase and displayed to a packed hall, in front of the cameras from all the Canadian television networks, were those given to me by the staff of the president of the United States, Bill Clinton. I took one in my hand and showed it to the judge, saying, "From Hope, Arkansas, William Jefferson Clinton, President of the United States"—"small-town cheap." After that I procured another ball and read, "From Crawford, Texas, George W. Bush, President of the United States"—"small-town cheap." Then, "From Manila, Fidel Ramos, president of the Philippines"—"small-town cheap." And to finish off, I brought out a ball from the law office Ogilvy Renaud, reminding everyone that this was the law firm of Brian Mulroney, of Bernard Roy, Mulroney's former principal secretary and the commission's lawyer, and of the daughter of Judge Gomery himself, but it would be non-sense, an oxymoron, to say "small-town cheap," because all three were citizens of the very bourgeois suburb of Westmount. Of course, this little demonstration inspired much hilarity all across the country, and I was quite happy with my performance. I still smile when I think of the article in the *Globe and Mail* by Margaret Wente, headed, "This man has balls," an expression whose double meaning and saucy irony was lost on no one.

When I was a student at Laval University, I participated actively in the 1956 provincial election, and as a young lawyer I did the same in the 1960 election. Among the young orators who supported the National Assembly member René Hamel, who later became justice minister under Jean Lesage, was a very colourful labour leader who was a Belgian immigrant. It was said of him that the first thing he did when he arrived in the port of Quebec, right after setting foot on the dock, was to ask the group who were there to meet him, "Who forms the government here?" To which the reply was, "Why are you asking this question, M. Vassart?" "Well, because I'm against, and I'd like to know against whom. . . ." John Diefenbaker was the Conservative prime minister of Canada and Antonio Barrette was premier of Quebec, elected under the banner of the Union Nationale. And so Vassart was very comfortable supporting the Liberals, who were in opposition at both levels of government. Mind you, after

Lesage's Liberals were elected in Quebec in 1960, and Pearson's at the federal level three years later, we never again saw hide nor hair of him.

It's not widely known, but Aline always had a good sense of humour, and the public became aware of this during the convention that chose my successor in November 2003, shortly after I retired from political life. During my forty years on the public stage, she rarely gave interviews to journalists. However, on this occasion she accepted an invitation from Peter Mansbridge of the CBC. During the conversation Mansbridge observed that she was not often seen on television or on the news, but that her husband, on the other hand, often talked about her when speaking in public. She shot back, "Jean is like Columbo, who's always talking about his wife!" Everyone on the set, cameramen included, burst out laughing. Mansbridge himself laughed so hard that he had to take a break before continuing the conversation.

One day during my years as prime minister, I was making my way to my room at the Hotel Shediac at the end of an exhausting day, and some journalists managed to corner me to ask questions. It was late, I was very tired, and one of them was particularly aggressive on the subject of my upcoming visit to China, asking me something like "What are you, as a Canadian democrat, going to say to the president of the authoritarian Chinese regime about human rights? Are you going to put this non-elected leader of his country of 1 billion 300 million Chinese, in his place?" I replied, "You want me, the prime minister of a country with a population of 35 million people, to tell him how to govern his country of 1 billion 300 million citizens, when it would be totally unacceptable if I were to dare tell the premier of Saskatchewan, for example, how to run his government? The prime minister of Canada must not interfere in the affairs of his provinces, but for China, that's okay!" For the Chinese this became the "Shediac declaration," and apparently they still remember it.

At the beginning of March 2018, I attended the funeral of Pierre Garceau, one of my best friends and a former classmate at college and university, who after a number of years practising law in Trois-Rivières was one of the first representatives of the Canadian International Development Association (CIDA) in Africa, then twice ambassador and commissioner for Federal Judicial Affairs. His wife, Angèle, asked me to say a few words at the church, and insisted I do so with humour. And so I recounted that when Pierre and I arrived at the Laval University Faculty of Law, we were vexed to discover that our classmates who were supporters of the Union Nationale had each received, free of charge, a copy of Quebec's Revised Statutes, while we, seen as Liberals, were asked to pay five dollars. Outraged, we called Premier Duplessis's secretary, the formidable Auréa

Cloutier, and she set up a meeting for us with her boss. A deft player, he received us, probably hoping to amuse himself a little at the expense of two plucky young students whose decidedly Liberal families were very prominent in the Mauricie region.

We told him that it was unfair to make us pay five dollars for something that was free for the others, when in principle we had the same rights. He replied that it was not a question of rights, but of privilege. To be a student at the university was a privilege, and not a right. Those who had the privilege of receiving the Revised Statutes free of charge were in fact privileged because they had faith . . . in the Union Nationale. After a long discussion concerning a society of law versus a society of privilege, laced with humour and political anecdotes, he finally said, "I'll give you two copies for the price of one." We'd taken up an hour of our premier's time to save $2.50 each. To reach that point required two cheeky young students and a premier with an undeniable sense of humour.

As Pierre loved to have fun, he wanted to say goodbye in his own way. And so, as his mortal remains left the church, his grandsons carried off his coffin to the accompaniment of Carlos Gradel's famous tango, "Por una cabeza." Once again the colourful Pierre had the last word, with a smile.

47

LORD CONRAD BLACK

In the book *Letters to Limbo*, written by Robert Laird Borden, the former prime minister outlines the circumstances under which he allowed a vote on a resolution by the Conservative MP W.F. Nickle, abolishing noble titles emanating from London. Borden asserted that in 1919 Canada was an independent nation with a status equal to that of Great Britain and no longer needed to be satisfied with crumbs from the British government's table. When I read this now one-hundred-year-old story about a Conservative prime minister, I couldn't help smiling and thinking back on the much publicized controversy that led Conrad Black to give up his Canadian citizenship in order to become a British lord.

On the way to the G8 summit in Cologne, Germany, in 1999, I was making an official visit to Vienna, Austria. Suddenly I received a telephone call, apparently very urgent, from the press magnate, Conrad Black. He was facing, he said, a very urgent problem that according to him required my immediate attention. As Black had acquired control of the Telegraph Group in London, the tradition of the English Conservative Party decreed that the head of the party recommend to Prime Minister Tony Blair that a seat be awarded him in the House of Lords. Respecting tradition, PM Tony Blair recommended to the Queen that she proceed with Conrad Black's appointment. When the Queen's staff, which had the right to name citizens to the upper chamber of the British Parliament, received this recommendation, they were astonished to see a Canadian on the list of future lords. It seems that in preceding years, certain members of the Weston family had refused this same honour because they did not want to give up their Canadian citizenship, as Lord Roy Herbert Thomson had done in 1964. This unforeseen development obliged Blair to inform Black that he could not proceed until the situation was clarified.

And so Black became desperate because, he told me, his appointment to the British House of Lords was to be announced publicly the next day. And he had scheduled a huge reception to celebrate the event on the following Saturday; the invitations had been sent out, and the champagne was already on ice. I felt that I was talking to someone who was at his wit's end, promising me heaven and earth to break the impasse. Poor me, I had no idea about those rules dating from 1919. I asked Black to give me a few hours to clarify the situation. The Privy Council informed me that there were strict rules on the matter, which had in fact been renewed by the Mulroney government. In light of this, Blair removed Black's name from the list and promised that everything would be put off until the end of the year. Black was furious, and I was very embarrassed, because I'd known him for a long time. Without ever being close, our relations had generally been amicable, but personally, I couldn't care less whether he became a lord or not.

To study the question, I asked the deputy prime minister, Herb Gray, to preside over a special cabinet committee that included the minister of foreign affairs, Lloyd Axworthy. Reading Prime Minister Pearson's memoirs, I learned that he'd had a discussion with his counterpart in Great Britain on the subject of the appointment of the president of the *Globe and Mail* to the British House of Lords. Roy Thomson had had to renounce his Canadian citizenship to become Lord Roy Thomson, Baron of Fleet. The title is hereditary, but his son Kenneth and his grandson David, who succeeded him as head of the Thomson empire, did not use the title in Canada and chose not to take their place in the British House of Lords, in order to avoid losing their Canadian citizenship. The report of the committee presided over by Herb Gray recommended to me that the guidelines established in 1919 by Robert L. Borden's Conservative government, which ruled out the existence of two classes of citizens in Canada, not be changed. In the end, Conrad Black preferred the crumbs from the British table to his Canadian citizenship, and he became Lord Black, Baron of Crossharbour.

When the decision of the very powerful Conrad Black to

surrender his Canadian citizenship, as Lord Roy Thomson had done before him, was made public, his Conservative friends attacked me most virulently. *The Globe and Mail* and the *National Post* called me a dictator and a man who had contempt for Anglo-Saxon culture, and the Conservative political class didn't spare me either. The worst is that Black decided to sue me personally before the courts, even though the recommendation came from a cabinet committee that was almost entirely anglophone. Aline became very nervous and fearful at the prospect of me being sued by such a wealthy man. I said to Aline, "Don't worry. It's the act of a desperate man." People like Conrad Black often try to intimidate by way of frivolous lawsuits. I've heard that his friend Donald Trump has the same habit, this fellow who had been subpoenaed to testify on Black's behalf at his trial in Chicago. As the saying goes, "Qui se ressemblent s'assemblent"—birds of a feather flock together!

For me everything worked out well, since the Ontario courts unanimously rejected Black's request (4-0), and I was not forced to sell my house and furniture to pay for a claim of that magnitude. On the other hand, the consequences for Lord Black couldn't have been more disastrous. When, a few years later, the American justice system hauled him before the courts, and he was found guilty of fraud along with two Canadians and an American, Black was sentenced to six and a half years in prison. The two Canadians asked to serve their sentences in Canada, which the Canadians were allowed to do by virtue of a treaty with the United States, but not Black, because he was no longer a Canadian national. The Canadians were also able to serve reduced time, and receive more lenient treatment than if they had stayed in the United States. They were released after only a few months, while Conrad Black still had to sweat out several years in an American prison—even though his sentence was reduced, on appeal. I don't know if he acknowledges the error he made in choosing a wig and crumbs from a British table over Canadian citizenship, but at least he was able to enjoy a number of years with no snow, and plenty of fresh oranges to savour, while he pondered it all in Florida behind bars.

48

SOME LITTLE-KNOWN IMPORTANT DECISIONS

I have often been asked about the most important decisions I had to make during my long career, and it is always
hard for me to reply. Some are well known, because controversial; I'm thinking of the decision not to join the coalition
that, unjustifiably in my opinion, threw itself into a war in
Iraq; or the Clarity Act, which was designed to ensure that
no referendum will be held here without rules of engagement
that are clear to both sides. To clean up our public finances
and bring them into a zone of budgetary equilibrium was
also a crucial decision that required a great deal of discipline
and determination on the part of the government and all
Canadians. Other decisions were equally important to me,
but they are little known, or not known at all. Let me tell you
about some of them.

In September 1976, I became the new minister of Canadian
Industry, Trade, and Commerce. Right away, as I always did, I

asked the officials what were the three most urgent problems. They told me that Canadair had an option to acquire the plans for building the Lear Star from the airplane manufacturer Lear, in Texas; the Star was a private plane for business people. As the option was expiring at the end of the month, this was an urgent matter.

The advisers to the department were divided, some thinking that it was a good idea to acquire these plans, and others holding the opposite opinion. So I decided to phone Bill Lear, and I asked him to give me three good reasons why Canadair should acquire his project. "First," he replied, "there is already a Lear jet on the market which is selling very well. The problem is, it's become too small for its natural clientele, the rich. The private jet has become the castle for the wealthy, and when you're rich you don't like to bend down to enter your castle. I think you need a free height of at least six feet from floor to ceiling, which means that the airplane body must be wider, also increasing the size of the fuel tank. As a result, the range of the plane will go from 2,500 to 5,000 miles, making possible a non-stop trip from Los Angeles to New York or from New York to London. As well, you'll have to find appropriate wings, and to support a broader airplane body, they will have to be of the 'critical wing' type, which is already in use on military aircraft in the United States. Once you have the body and the wings for the plane, you'll need motors, and I recommend Lycoming, which are already on the market. It's a matter of putting together those three elements, as simple as that!"

He continued the conversation by asking me to open *Time* magazine to page 40. I did so, and he went on, "You see, Ford is bringing out a new car model, and to show off its modern new design, they photographed their automobile beside a Lear jet that I designed twenty-five years ago." Everything he said was clear, direct, unpretentious—and therefore convincing.

Meanwhile, the federal government had taken over Canadair from General Dynamics, which wanted to shut the company down because US rules did not allow it to repair American-built military planes in Canada. As a result, the company had on order for construction only planes for extinguishing forest fires, which was not enough to ensure its profitability. The federal government was under pressure to act in order to avoid the shutdown of Canadair. I therefore decided to buy the Lear Star option, which became the Challenger. Having done so, we saved Canadair, and instead of disappearing as General Dynamics had decided, Canadair became a division of Bombardier Aeronautics. The aeronautics sector, as a result, became the largest industrial employer in Canada, with more than 50,000 workers.

This success earned me the thanks of the Bombardier employees' union, which named me honorary president. What is more, during the 1993 electoral campaign, when I was contesting my first election as leader of the Liberal Party, the employees gave me an enthusiastic reception at one of the Bombardier factories in Ville St-Laurent. It was a terrific boost from the workers, at the start of an electoral campaign that led me to become the prime minister of Canada. I thank them once again from the bottom of my heart.

In the years 1972 and 1973, as the world energy crisis bore down, many participants in the oil consortium Syncrude Canada began to abandon ship, including Atlantic Richfield and Shell Global. In particular, they found the Alberta government too greedy in demanding the equivalent of 50 percent of the extraction rights. When Shell Canada also began to waver, Peter Lougheed asked the federal government for help in preventing a work stoppage on this gigantic project. A meeting was organized in Winnipeg; Premier Lougheed participated, along with several Albertan ministers, Premier Bill Davis of Ontario, federal energy minister Donald Macdonald, and myself as president of the Treasury Board of Canada.

The meeting started badly. Shell stated right off the bat that it would no longer participate, and the position of my friend Don Macdonald didn't really please Peter Lougheed. Lougheed was a smart man who expressed his ideas clearly and strongly, and the federal energy minister was the same type, which of course made sparks fly. After two hours the meeting, deadlocked, had to be adjourned, and for the next two hours or more, I found myself shuttling back and forth between the Alberta contingent, Bill Davis representing Ontario, and Don Macdonald speaking for the Department of Energy, Mines, and Resources. By the end of the day, all the parties had arrived at the necessary compromises for Syncrude's pivotal project to survive.

Syncrude was the first extraction project for Alberta's oil sands and marked the beginning of that province's forty years of considerable prosperity. When I left political life in 2004, I was asked to work part-time in the big law firm Bennett Jones in Calgary, and when I arrived there for the first time I was greeted by the office's principal adviser, Peter Lougheed himself. He declared, in front of a group of journalists, that if there had been an agreement on that famous February 3, 1975, it was in large part thanks to my actions in the corridors of the hotel where we were staying. I thought this was overstating the case somewhat, but clearly I was happy to hear the most impressive Alberta premier I've known acknowledge the role played by the federal government in his province's energy sector.

Unfortunately, there are not many citizens of this rich Western province who remember, or want to remember, what the funds of the federal and Ontario governments did to save their oil industry during the difficult 1970s, at the height of the world energy crisis.

When I announced in 2002 that Canada was going to ratify the Kyoto Protocol, those who opposed it accused me of having made the decision on my own, and strictly speaking, it was true. They were absolutely right. The caucus was in large majority favourable, but the pro-business MPs and ministers opposed it, claiming that it would be impossible for Canada to reach the targets specified by the Protocol. I myself thought that it would be very difficult to succeed. During the required twenty hours in the plane heading for South Africa and an international conference where the subject was to be discussed, I had a lot of time to think. I remained very concerned about Canada's inability to take a clear position on a subject so crucial to the future of humanity. I knew that it would be practically impossible for Canada to reach 100 percent of the objectives; at best we might reach 80 percent. On the other hand, if I said yes to ratification of the Protocol, and we made it to 80 percent, that was much better than zero. Not perfect, but to do nothing at all seemed to me totally irresponsible. And so when my turn came to speak the next day, I announced that we were going to ratify Kyoto.

As soon as I was home, I went to Alberta to explain to the oil industry that it would be best to adjust to the new reality bit by bit. Thanks to the help of Murray Edwards, the Canadian superstar of that industry in Alberta, and to the federal cabinet secretary, Alex Himelfarb, we were able to reach an agreement with the industry. Evidently the business people would have preferred to keep to the status quo with me, and then, later, to persuade Paul Martin and Stephen Harper to back off, which they succeeded in doing. Fortunately though, when Justin Trudeau became prime minister, he reversed the position of his two predecessors and signed the Paris Protocol. All of which proves that very often in public life, things go one step forward, two steps back, then another one forward again.

This reminds me of something else that caused a lot of stir at the time. Under Brian Mulroney's government, at the height of the furor created by the often acrimonious discussions surrounding the Meech and Charlottetown constitutional agreements, neither of which came to fruition, we were told that if Quebec was not recognized in the Constitution as a distinct society, it would be the end of the world.

Much to the annoyance of the intellectuals, journalists, and politicians on all sides, I summed up the situation with a typically Canadian metaphor, declaring that there was no point in getting all excited, since we were simply stuck in the snow.

What do Canadians do in such a situation? They don't get all worked up. A little nudge to the front, a little nudge to the back, don't spin your wheels in butter; maintain contact with the ground—and eventually you'll find yourself back on the road.

The right-thinking people rending their garments over a constitutional quagmire laid into me in no uncertain terms, and at times even insulted me for saying something that was apparently too down-to-earth. More than twenty-five years have passed. The "distinct society" is not in the Constitution, and Quebec and the rest of Canada continue their marriage of convenience in a land that is still the envy of the world.

49

POLITICAL FOES AND FRIENDS

As you must have some interest in public life if you are reading these pages, you will understand that it is the extreme political partisanship we are now witnessing, particularly in the United States, that leads me to talk to you about the relationship between two people who faced off in the House of Commons for decades: Joe Clark, MP, minister, and Progressive Conservative prime minister; and your humble servant: MP, minister, and Liberal prime minister.

When Joe Clark became an MP in 1972, he was my opposition critic for Northern Development, while another newly elected MP, Flora MacDonald, was my critic for Indian Affairs. These two new MPs kept themselves in shape at my expense. They were both very articulate, and I had to defend myself tooth and nail. It's interesting to note that we all had prominent careers later on. Flora became minister of foreign affairs in 1979 and was the first woman to hold this important post; Joe became the Progressive Conservative leader in 1976, prime minister in 1979, and minister of foreign affairs under Mulroney. As for me, you'd have to think that the blows inflicted by Flora and Joe in the House of Commons helped me to become a better politician, because as of 1974 Prime Minister Trudeau appointed me six times to the cabinet. Subsequently, I was leader of the Liberal Party, and prime minister of Canada for ten years. Often, to tease Joe, I tell him that I called him and his colleague Flora and Fauna.

Several weeks before Joe Clark became leader of the Progressive Conservatives, I asked him what was going to happen at the leadership convention called to replace the retiring leader, Robert Stanfield, and he replied that it was impossible to foresee. So I asked him if he himself was going to be a candidate, and he said no. I told him that he should present himself, because being young he had nothing to lose; he came from Western Canada; he was viewed as a moderate in Ontario; and he was bilingual, rare for a PC member from the West. I ended my monologue by telling him that he certainly wouldn't win if he wasn't a candidate.

After his victory I sent him a letter of congratulations, and I told him that I had won twenty dollars betting on his victory. He wrote to thank me for my good wishes, and also for the excellent advice I gave him concerning the leadership, and asked me in passing if there was something for him in the twenty dollars. A few days later I ran into him in the House of Commons and gave him ten dollars, telling him that he well deserved it. To tease him, I told him that I'd given him the advice in the interests of the Liberals and not the Conservatives. He replied, "We'll see," and he was right, because in the next election he defeated Pierre Trudeau and became the sixteenth prime minister of Canada. Joe and I crossed swords from 1972 to 2003, over thirty-one years, and when we had occasion to meet, we enjoyed talking together, and I considered him to be one of my friends.

Some would be astonished to learn that I also had very cordial relations with the notorious Pierre Bourgault, who at the time had founded the Rassemblement pour l'indépendance nationale (RIN), the most radical separatist party in Quebec. I remember a debate between the unelected Quebec lieutenant of Robert Stanfield in Quebec, Marcel Faribault, and myself on the one side, and on the other side two pro-separatist participants, one of whom was Pierre Bourgault. Bourgault did not mince words, saying that all federal Liberal MPs were jerks. Which did not exactly please me. Later in the debate, M. Faribault, who was a prominent businessman, said something that was unfortunately inexact, and I politely corrected him. When Bourgault had the floor again, after having noted my correction, he withdrew his earlier comments, confessing that after all, it wasn't true that all Liberal MPs were jerks, not me in any case.

As I always called those who advocated independence separatists, the higher-ups in the Parti Québécois accused me of not speaking good French because I called them separatists rather then "indépendantistes" or sovereignists. As for him, Pierre Bourgault told me, "When you call me a goddamn separatist, that doesn't shock me, because I am a separatist." And I replied, "When you call me a goddamn federalist, that doesn't shock me, because I am a goddamn federalist."

After the 1995 referendum, Bourgault made a declaration that greatly surprised me: "We have only one great obstacle to overcome before we succeed in separating: Chrétien is not yet dead."

Often, talking with friends, I said that Bourgault's approach would have been far more dangerous than Claude Morin's step-by-step strategy or the hedging of René Lévesque. Where the future of a separate Quebec was concerned, Bourgault said, essentially, "We'll probably be poorer for ten years, but if we roll up our sleeves we can get over the hurdles, and in a decade we'll be America's francophone Sweden." One night one of my friends said to me, "Stop, Jean! You're starting to convince us. . . ."

Shortly before his death, in a conversation with Marie-France Bazzo on Radio-Canada, Bourgault told her that he had heard me in an interview with George Stephanopoulos on the American network ABC, talking about the war in Iraq. What I said had impressed him so much that he admitted that if I were a candidate in the next election, he would probably vote for Jean Chrétien. Bazzo replied, "Many people would have heart attacks if they heard that Pierre Bourgault would vote for Jean Chrétien!" Bourgault replied, "Not only am I saying it, but I've already published it. . . ." From a founder of the RIN, who could ask for more?

After talking about a Conservative leader and a separatist leader, I'll complete the picture with a story about a good friend who began as a strong adversary and became an able collaborator: the New Democrat Roy Romanow. In 1980 he was the attorney general of Saskatchewan and the spokesperson for the provinces in the post-referendum discussions that led us to patriate the Constitution and give Canadians a charter of constitutional rights. After the referendum, all during the summer of 1980, the ministers of justice and those of federal-provincial relations had meetings almost every week in different provinces. And every Friday, Roy Romanow, as spokesperson for the provinces, and myself, as spokesperson for the federal government, held a press conference to give a progress report on our work. The journalists called us Uke and Tuque—Uke referring to Roy's Ukrainian origins, and Tuque to my regional French-Canadian roots. At the end of the constitutional talks that lasted two years, we, along with Ontario's justice minister, Roy McMurtry, were the ones who worked out a solution enabling us to bring home the Constitution from London, and to give Canadians a constitution that was authentically Canadian, with a Charter of Rights that revolutionized Canadian law.

As I liked to hear opinions that went beyond the people around me and the advisers who breathed the air of Parliament Hill every day, I had a list of fifteen contacts from all across Canada whom I called on a regular basis. Their opinions were essential to me to ensure that I was on the right path. Even if Romanow was a New Democrat, he was always high on the list of those anonymous and indispensable advisers. Twenty years after my election as prime minister, not three weeks went by without Uke and Tuque talking. Two politicians of different stripes who became very good friends.

For Joe Clark, Pierre Bourgault, Roy Romanow, and Jean Chrétien, it was possible to play hard on the political skating rink, and then get together for a beer once the game was over.

CONCLUSION

Whanhen I began to write the stories you have just read, I thought that only members of my family would have access to these pages, and my aim was to show them that it's possible to take one's work seriously without taking oneself too seriously. Humour in politics is one of the resources I've drawn on freely in the course of my career. Not always successfully, I must admit, but more often than not, it has been well received, as you've been able to witness throughout this book.

I thought this was important, now that we've been plunged into a new world of instant news, unfiltered and not always trustworthy, which constantly assails us on social media. While news took a whole day, or even a week, to circulate at the beginning of my career in 1963, today bad news is instantly flashed over five continents. Good news, on the other hand, rarely makes the headlines. Still, it's important to put everything into perspective, and I've had the privilege of looking back over fifty-five years, following my election as a federal member of Parliament in the same year, 1963, that

Lester B. Pearson became the country's prime minister. Over all those years I have no clear memory of a single day when I opened a newspaper, watched or listened to a news report, to find it stated that things were getting better in the world.

And yet, in the preface to her 2015 report, the head of the United Nations Development Programme, Helen Clark, underlined the impressive progress made in the field of human development over the last twenty-five years.

She wrote, in part: "Today we are living longer, more children are being educated, and a larger number of people have access to clean water and basic hygiene. Individual income around the world has grown, while poverty has diminished, raising many people's standard of living. The computer revolution has forged links between individuals from different countries and societies. Work has contributed to this progress by developing the skills of each individual. Decent work has contributed to human dignity and opened the door to every individual's full participation in society."

This is rather good news, where international development is concerned. What's more, since World War II the number of armed conflicts in the world has steadily decreased, even though, of course, they still exist. Finally, in the context of the 1980s push for a "Star Wars" missile defence system, the planetary stock of nuclear arms has gradually shrunk after having reached unprecedented heights at the end of the last century. The threat is still there, but our collective capacity to control it has significantly improved.

The same thing applies to anti-personnel mines, whose

stocks continue to diminish, thanks to the Ottawa Treaty signed in 1997 by more than 120 countries. The progress is remarkable, but there too, nothing is perfect, as major countries such as the United States, China, India, and Russia have not yet signed the document.

Terrorist attacks all over the world, especially in Europe, still dominate news reports, sometimes for weeks. Long after the events, the media have us reliving the horrors. The phenomenon, however, is not new. Outbreaks of terrorism have been occurring sporadically here and there since the 1960s. Who remembers the FLQ here at home, the Red Army Faction, also known as the Baader-Meinhof gang, in Germany, the Red Brigades in Italy, Action Directe in France, the IRA in Northern Ireland, the Shining Path in Peru, etc.?

These groups have had their day, and we have together overcome the terror they left behind them, as we will surmount that sown by today's terrorists, notably Al-Qaeda and Daesh, or the so-called Islamic State.

Meanwhile, here in Canada, what have we done to develop our country since the 1960s? Well, we have created a universal system of health care, which, yes, is regularly called into question, but which we would not abandon for anything in the world. We have established a system of old age pensions for all, which must, there too, be readjusted as the country's demographic evolves. This is another instance of collective progress whose details must always be revised, but not the basic principle of offering proper protection to all citizens towards the end of their lives.

We have repatriated our Constitution and added a Charter of Rights and Freedoms that is the envy of many peoples who cherish democracy. The death sentence has been abolished. Abortion is no longer illegal, and can be performed in full security, protecting women's health. Marriage between same sex partners is no longer a contentious issue, but rather a reality consistent with equal rights for all. And now it is possible to obtain medical aid in order to die with dignity, shortening unbearable suffering when the outcome is not in doubt.

All these instances bear witness to undeniable progress towards a world that is more egalitarian, and that bears the stamp of greater humanity. I believe that the task of a leader in today's world is in large part to remind us of where we started from, in order to demonstrate the great distance we have come. This is not a matter of self-congratulation, but rather of recognizing all we have been able to achieve over the last fifty years, to give ourselves new strength and the will to meet the many challenges, ever more complex, that are facing us.

The responsibility of any true leader is to create a positive and optimistic atmosphere, an atmosphere that suggests that the best is yet to come; that gives to each of us the desire to prevail, and to reach goals that are forward-looking and ambitious. This is not to underestimate the difficulties involved, but to avoid discouragement and to be able to forge ahead with determination and self-confidence.

The leader who succeeds in that frees up around him

extraordinary energy and dynamism; the sort of energy that, in the long run, enables us to move mountains. That is what I have tried to do all my life.

When I took stock of my decade as prime minister and head of government, there was only one question to be asked: Did I leave the country in better shape than I found it? That will always be a subject for debate, but in the end, I sincerely believe that Canada was better off in 2003 than in 1993.

In fact, when we took power in October 1993, the *Wall Street Journal* wrote that Canada had become almost a Third World country, but in the autumn of 2003, on the contrary, *The Economist* declared "Canada Is Cool," highlighting what in its opinion was the remarkable progress made by Canada under my administration. In so doing, *The Economist* endorsed the conclusions of the annual United Nations report that over ten years placed Canada eight times at the top of its global standing for quality of life. That being said, our country represents an ideal that is young, unfinished, and the bearer of immense aspirations, to which succeeding governments must respond as best they can, and with inspiration, in accordance with the challenges that prevail in their time.

All Canadians deserve credit for our accomplishments. They made the necessary choices; they supported our policies and put forth the effort that was needed for the recovery of our country when it was weakened and its public finances were in tatters.

And so I conclude this book the same way I ended most of my speeches, affirming that there are millions of men and women across the globe who would give all they have to come and share in our presumed troubles, because they know that Canada is a land of tolerance, of sharing, of generosity, of respect for all origins, languages, religions, skin colours, and human rights. And yes, life is beautiful here. We can dream, and we can achieve our dreams.

Vive le Canada!

A TOAST BY

MONSIEUR JACQUES CHIRAC
PRESIDENT OF THE REPUBLIC

ON THE OCCASION OF A DINNER OFFERED
IN HONOUR OF THE RIGHT HONOURABLE
PRIME MINISTER OF CANADA
AND MADAME ALINE CHRÉTIEN

* * *

PALAIS DES AFFAIRES ÉTRANGÈRES—PARIS

TUESDAY 9 DECEMBER 2003

Mr. Prime Minister, my dear Jean,
My dear Aline,

Welcoming you to Paris is for my wife and me a pleasure,
an honour, and a most happy event. A visit to France by
the prime minister of Canada is always a momentous and
stirring occasion. For the French, Canada is the immense
country, the infinite land of promise, which holds a special
place in our hearts. It is the memory of a glorious episode

in our national history that, sadly, left a deep wound when ended. And it is a community whose fidelity to its origins, when it was left to itself two and a half centuries ago, enabled it to prosper, to assume its place as Canadian, and yet to remain French in spite of history—this hope, this dream of America, forever renewed.

My dear Jean, you are one of the most important authors of this success, this modernity. Your visit comes at a significant time, since you have decided, alas, to retire. This evening I want to express my regret at seeing you step away from those duties that you have carried out so admirably—although the word itself is inadequate, the judgment is shared by the entire world and those who preside over it—but above all I want to express my admiration and my gratitude for your accomplishments and for the tasks we have undertaken together.

To say that your career has been extraordinary is an understatement: your forty years of public life, three successive mandates as prime minister, to which you committed your impressive gifts as a man and a leader. You defended with tenacity and intelligence your vision of Canada, of its place in America, its place in world affairs. You made decisions out of conviction, under the most difficult circumstances: this I witnessed on more than one occasion.

What you have accomplished in the service of your country, and the message it has sent out into the world, is inspiring. There is hardly a sphere in which you have not made your mark. As a tribute to our shared passion for the First Peoples, in particular the Inuit, and in recalling the memorable journey during which you introduced me to the splendours of the Far North, allow me to speak of your contribution as minister of Indian Affairs and Northern Development. Your mission then was to help assure for the members of the First Nations a life marked by dignity and the full possession of their rights. And you are one of the few statesmen on this planet to have assumed that responsibility and to have done so with effectiveness and dignity. This deserves recognition, and it is a reflection of your particularly generous heart and your impassioned intelligence.

Prime Minister, you have presided over a process in the course of which the constitutional consensus of your country has been reaffirmed following an exemplary series of negotiations.

Under your guidance, Canada found its way back to a balanced budget, to growth, and to the creation of jobs in a world that, alas, was experiencing its share of problems and economic and societal difficulties. Canada's impressive performance placed it in the highest rank of the G8 countries, and that was your doing. This striking success owes much to the courageous measures you took, notably to reform the State and to restore its budgetary health. The results you obtained in these areas command our admiration, because they are unequalled.

On the international stage your actions—and to this I can bear witness—have been consistent with the values

Canada embodies: diversity, solidarity, peace. I would
like in particular to commend you for your contribution
to the Francophonie both in Canada and internationally.

Our world today is in need of security, and that demands
both justice and stability. I am proud that we have so
often found ourselves side by side in international
forums to promote the primacy of law, the importance
of multilateralism, and the responsibility to reach out
to the neediest among us. Speaking for myself, I have
always derived great satisfaction from working with
you in a spirit of friendship and collaboration, pursuing
a goal shared by our two nations: that of a world in
which tolerance, equality, and humanism would prevail.

We are both committed to the achievement of this
goal. By steadfastly defending our positions regarding
sustainable development. By combating global warming
through the ratification, despite difficulties, despite
opposition, of the indispensable Kyoto Protocol. By
working towards the responsible conduct of international
trade and the financial markets. By promoting, steadfastly,
the new idea that is the defence of cultural diversity,
an endeavour in which we have been able, together,
to enlist the support of the Francophonie and UNESCO.
By together supporting the creation of the International
Criminal Court and the universal banning of antipersonnel
mines. In making common cause, maintaining and
strengthening the central role the United Nations
must play in conflict resolution and international crises.

In committing our armed forces on the ground to the service of peace in Bosnia, in Afghanistan, in Ituri. In working in support of Africa, to which we both became very committed when initiating an important partnership with NEPAD at Kananaskis, during the historic G8 summit, under your presidency. And while at times we had our differences, they were always dealt with in the spirit of confidence and friendship that marks our relationship.

Prime Minister, my dear Jean, Canada is for France much more than a partner, much more than an ally. Ardent and profound, marked by the close ties between our peoples, our relationship has, over ten years, under your impetus, grown in strength and intensity. And now I would like very simply to thank you, with profound gratitude, for all you have done.

Together, we have just visited at the Parc de la Villette the wonderful exhibition devoted to Canada today and to its modernity. It demonstrates just how much your country has transformed itself into a true model for the other developed countries in the community of nations. Canada has invested greatly in its youth, education, research, and new technologies. You yourself have been deeply involved in this enterprise.

At the same time, this great exhibition is a send-off for the events that throughout the year 2004 will mark the four-hundredth anniversary of the arrival of Samuel de Champlain in Canada.

This first European settlement in a distant land would be followed, four years later, by the founding of Quebec, which we will celebrate in 2008.

It was the beginning of a very long friendship between France and Canada.

On both sides of the Atlantic a bond was forged that nothing, neither distance nor tragedies, nor the errors and accidents of history, could ever undo. Amid misfortunes, the steadfast loyalty of the French and their descendants in Canada was rooted in their attachment to our common language. Through their perseverance, they bound their country to this bilingualism, this cultural dialogue that today represents the essence of its strength, its genius, its very nature. And thanks to you I was able, on the occasion of the francophone summit in Moncton, to celebrate in Memramcook the unwavering bonds between France and the Acadians.

This cooperation, this difficult but fertile cultural adventure, this dialogue between anglophones and francophones, has extended today to the cultures and languages of the First Nations that Canada has fully recognized on your initiative and under your leadership. They are further enriched by the thousands of new arrivals, women and men of all origins, come from everywhere in the world to fulfil their potential and remake their lives thanks to this comradeship that we encounter too rarely elsewhere. The great Canadian cities, brimming with energy and vitality, bear vivid witness to this multicultural energy.

Every day, Canada, a land of multiplicity, a land of differences, cultivates and refines, in tolerance and peace, the pleasures of living together. On every occasion it favours all the promise, all the richness, of the Other. And in that way, I believe that Canada is fully engaged in this century. It is living proof that diversity is a measure of openness and success.

Finally, it is to you both, my dear Jean, my dear Aline, that I want to pay tribute on the occasion of this evening of friendship.

At the end of a long and brilliant career, during which Aline has been your companion in good times and bad, a career that has given you little rest, little time, a new life is opening for you both. Bernadette joins with me in wishing you much, much happiness. I am not totally convinced that it will last very long, this repose. But that is another problem.

It is to your happiness, dear Jean, dear Aline, that I raise my glass, in honour of an exceptional and highly esteemed statesman, who has written some powerful and beautiful pages in the history of his country and the world, and in honour of his wife to whom I pay a respectful and affectionate tribute. I raise it, my dear Jean, to the future of Canada. I raise it to the unbreakable bond between Canada and France.

Vive le Canada,
Vive la France.

ACKNOWLEDGEMENTS

I am most grateful to my friend Patrick Parisot, Canadian ambassador to Cuba, and to his partner, Carmen Altamirano, my first readers, researchers and editors. For more than a year, they were patient and generous enough to accompany me on this journey, notably in checking dates and places.

I would like to thank Catherine Clark, for persuading her father, Joe Clark, to do the special favour of writing the foreword to this book. I thank him most sincerely.

I would also like to thank Louise Crête-Dandurand, Angèle Neveu-Garceau, John Rae, Eddie Goldenberg, Yves Gougoux, Alain Garceau, Bruce Hartley, and Denise Labelle. All read my manuscript and shared their helpful observations.

Thanks to photographer Jean-Marc Carisse, whose images enliven this text.

Finally, my gratitude goes to Jean-François Bouchard and Pierre Cayouette of Éditions La Presse, as well as to Pamela Murray of Random House Canada. As well, thanks to Sheila Fischman and Donald Winkler for their excellent work in translating the French text into English.

And my particular thanks to my dear wife, Aline, for her legendary patience and her observations that were, as always, useful and valuable.

PHOTO CREDITS

All photographs by Jean-Marc Carisse / (Jean Chrétien Fonds, LAC), (Jean-Marc Carisse Fonds, LAC) and photos © Jean-Marc Carisse, with the following exceptions:

First insert, page i, top photo, and second insert, page ix, top photo: courtesy Jean Chrétien.

First insert, pages ii and iii: Murray Mosher

Second insert, page iv, middle photo and pages x and xi: Diana Murphy / Fonds Jean Chrétien / LAC

Second insert, page xii, bottom photo: The Canadian Press / Jonathan Hayward

Second insert, page xiii, bottom photo: Ivanoh Demers / *La Presse*

Second insert, page xv: Bruce Hartley

The Rt. Hon. JEAN CHRÉTIEN was first elected to Parliament in 1963, at the age of twenty-nine. Four years later he was given his first cabinet post and, over the next thirty years, he headed nine key ministries. From 1993 to 2003 he served as Canada's twentieth prime minister, winning three consecutive Liberal majority governments. He is the recipient of multiple honorary doctorates and is a Companion of the Order of Canada. In 2008 he became co-president of the InterAction Council, and in 2009 he was awarded the Order of Merit by Her Majesty Elizabeth II.

In 2014, he joined the law firm Dentons as counsel, working primarily in Ottawa.